Great Responsibi

by

i

ACKNOWLEDGEMENTS

Dr. Dershem gratefully acknowledges the support of the South Central College administration and the MinnState system. *Great Responsibility* was written during a sabbatical from his teaching duties.

Table of Contents

INTRODUCTION

Modern Gods

"Superhero stories woke me up to my own potential. They gave me the basis of a code of ethics I still live by. By offering role models whose heroism and transcendent qualities would once have been haloed and clothed in floaty robes, they nurtured in me a sense of the cosmic and ineffable ... I had no need for faith. My gods were real, made of paper and light ..."
- Grant Morrison, *Supergods*

Comic-book superheroes have been described as the "gods" of the modern world. Although superheroes aren't worshiped, they *are* larger-than-life characters with extraordinary abilities who have epic adventures – and, importantly, serve as moral examples. Like the gods of ancient Greece and Rome, they possess superhuman powers and wage a never-ending war against the forces of evil. They also resemble those ancient deities in their imperfections. Superheroes are afflicted with the same flaws and face many of the same challenges as ordinary humans. They struggle with temptation, debate difficult decisions, and are wracked with guilt for failing the people they love. Of course, being superheroes, they also deal with problems all their own: unnatural disasters, alien invasions, villainous plots to conquer the world, etc. Still, no matter how fantastic the scenario, we can still identify with these characters. In the ways that matter most, they're just as human as the rest of us.

Of course, they're not "real" in a literal sense, but they do exist in the imaginations of the authors, artists, filmmakers and fans who create and consume them. In spite of their superhuman abilities, superheroes (and villains) can illustrate and exemplify what it means to be *human*. They're confronted with profound moral choices from the moment they decide to don a costume. *Should I be a hero or a villain? What am I fighting for, and why?* In many cases, their origin story provides their motivation and determines the kind of hero they become. Peter Parker (**Spider-Man**) initially used his powers for personal gain and failed to stop a fleeing criminal, who later killed Peter's beloved Uncle Ben. He never forgot the lesson his Uncle had taught him: "With great power comes great responsibility." As a child, Bruce Wayne witnessed the murder of his parents. Tormented by this trauma, he transformed himself into the **Batman**, a symbol of justice rising above the crime-ridden streets of Gotham City.

NOTE: The origins of many comic-book characters have been modified over the years due to "reboots," which simplify and streamline the fictional history of superhero universes. There are also differences between the biographies of comic-book superheroes and their small-screen (television) or big-screen (cinematic) equivalents. Although details differ, the broad strokes usually remain the same. For example, Superman is always a survivor of the doomed planet Krypton who was raised by adoptive Earth parents and fights on behalf of truth and justice. In my brief biographies of superheroes and villains, I'll try to summarize these common themes without getting bogged down in unnecessary details.

Batman (DC, 1939). Born into a family of great wealth in Gotham City, Bruce Wayne was struck by tragedy at a young age when his beloved parents were murdered in front of him. Raised by his loyal butler Alfred, Bruce dedicated his life to protecting the innocent. As a young man he traveled widely, training his body and mind until he achieved physical and mental perfection. Bruce returned to Gotham and adopted the symbol of the bat to strike fear into the hearts of superstitious criminals. As the Batman, he has protected his city and its inhabitants from countless nefarious villains. In addition to joining the Justice League, Batman has mentored many younger heroes, including Batgirl and several different Robins. Batman refuses to carry a gun, relying on "batarangs" and other nonlethal weapons instead. Although he lacks superpowers, he has access to advanced technology (including vehicles like the Batmobile) and is an extremely accomplished martial artist. ⊗

Spider-Man (Marvel, 1962). Peter Parker was visiting a science laboratory with his high school class when he was bitten by a radioactive spider. After discovering that he had gained amazing abilities, he created a costume and entered a wresting competition to win money. He encountered a fleeing burglar after a match. Although Peter could have very easily stopped the thief, he fatefully decided to let the man go. Later the same night the burglar killed Peter's Uncle Ben, who had been raising the young man along with his

Aunt May. Peter was devastated by the loss, consumed by guilt for his failure to act. From that day forward, he vowed to follow the lesson Ben had taught him before dying. As Spider-Man, he uses his spider-like abilities to fight crime and protect the people he loves. Spider-Man has been assisted by many different allies over the years (including two clones of Peter who became heroes in their own right) and has been an on-and-off member of the Avengers. He possesses enhanced strength, speed and agility, and has a "spider-sense" which warns him of imminent danger. Peter is a scientific genius who has invented many technologies, including "web-shooters" he uses to incapacitate criminals and swing through the streets of New York City. ⊗

Those of us in the real world are obviously unlikely to be bitten by a radioactive spider or inherit a manor house with a massive cave in the basement. However, we do face the same kinds of moral questions superheroes encounter in the course of their adventures. *What kind of person should I be? What motivates me? What are my deepest values? How do I balance my obligations to the people I love with the demands of my job and my duty to help people in need? Is it ever acceptable to lie or break the law to achieve a greater good?* The stakes may be lower in the choices we make – the fate of the world doesn't depend on whether I go to work today or decide to stay home and watch Netflix – but the questions can be just as challenging. When we're faced with difficult ethical decisions, most of us act on the basis of our conscience – which reflects our moral character – rather than thinking deeply about the problem. The same is true of superheroes; comic book "thought bubbles" rarely feature philosophical analysis of the ethical dimensions of their actions. They punch first and ask questions later. However, the tools of ethical thinking can help them (and us!) when we confront tough moral questions.

REAL-LIFE SUPERHEROES? Inspired by their fictional counterparts, individuals in cities around the world have attempted to become "actual" superheroes. According to news reports, they are dozens of these costumed do-gooders in the U.S. alone. Phoenix Jones (aka Ben Fodor) is one of the best known. Trained in mixed martial arts, he wears a colorful Kevlar uniform when patrolling the streets of Seattle. He decided to adopt a superhero persona after his car was burglarized and he witnessed a friend being assaulted outside a bar.

Although Jones has intervened in violent altercations on numerous occasions, his main goal is crime prevention. City authorities have described him as "deeply misguided" — a common reaction among people in law enforcement, who are concerned that vigilantes lack the proper training and may interfere with legitimate police work. Jones was arrested once for using pepper spray to break up a fight but was released without being charged. ⊗

Navigating the Book

Most books about morality use technical terms for ethical theories and concepts, which can be very intimidating to the uninitiated. It can be equally intimidating to encounter the world of superheroes for the first time; there's a lot of backstory which writers, artists and filmmakers assume the audience knows. To make the ethical ideas I'll be discussing as accessible as possible, I've tried to minimize my use of philosophical "jargon" (specialized words) within the main text. However, each chapter will include text boxes that define technical terms and provide brief biographies of relevant philosophers. They will be marked with the symbol for the Greek letter phi: ϕ. Likewise, the book will feature short introductions to superheroes and villains (usually the first time they're mentioned, sometimes later in the book if the characters are discussed there at greater length) for readers who are unfamiliar with this modern mythology. Examples will be drawn from the Marvel and DC Universes, which are by far the most popular comic-book franchises, and will be marked with this symbol: ⊗.

I'll frequently move back and forth between fictional illustrations of moral principles and real-world problems, which may strike some readers as jarring or even offensive. (How can the treatment of mutants in the Marvel Universe be compared to the mass killing of Jews in the Holocaust?) This is *not* meant to trivialize the serious issues being addressed. Instead, I hope the super-heroic examples will provide a novel perspective on controversial topics, enabling readers to understand them in a different way. In some cases, they might help us think more clearly about difficult issues by helping us avoid reflexive emotional reactions. For example, you might react very strongly to any mention of race-based discrimination, but you probably won't be affected in the same way by a discussion of how mutants are treated in the Marvel Universe. In other cases, superheroes can illustrate moral challenges in an amplified and thought-provoking way. For instance, we all strive to achieve the proper balance between acting in our own self-interest and helping others. Imagine that you possessed virtually unlimited power. Every second you spent relaxing, someone somewhere was dying – a fate you could have easily prevented!

A note on spoilers: Spoilers abound in this book, usually for comic-book plots that are years or decades old. Reader beware!

What is a comic book? Comic books are a form of literature that uses sequential art to tell stories. Although comics featuring super-powered heroes and villains are the best known, the medium has also been used to tell far more serious stories. For example, Art Spiegelman's graphic novel *Maus* is set in a concentration camp during the Holocaust. The history of mainstream comic books is usually divided into different periods, including the Golden Age of the 1930s and 40s, the Silver Age (1950s and 60s), the Bronze Age (1970s and 80s) and the Modern Age (mid-1980s to the present). The popularity of comics has waxed and waned over the decades, with two dominant companies – **Marvel** and **DC** – vying for supremacy. Characters originally created for comic books have become extraordinarily popular in other media such as television, film and video games. **❓ Have you ever read comic books? If not, are you familiar with superheroes from their representation in other media? Do you have any favorite heroes (or villains)?**

What is a superhero? A superhero is a person with extraordinary abilities who uses his or her skill to fight crime and serve the cause of justice. Most heroes (like **Superman** and Spider-Man) have superhuman powers, like incredible strength, flight, the ability to stick to walls, etc. Others (like Batman and Hawkeye) are "ordinary" humans who have undergone extensive training. Some heroes belong to teams that are officially sanctioned by the government (e.g., the **Justice League** and the **Avengers**), but most are vigilantes who operate outside the law. Super-heroes are inevitably opposed by super-villains, extraordinary individuals who use their abilities for personal gain, world domination, etc. Heroes also fight among themselves rather frequently, usually due to misunderstandings but occasionally because of actual ethical disagreements. ⊗

❷ Although comic books themselves are no longer read very widely – they were much more popular in the past – superhero characters have been incredibly successful in television, film and video games. How would you account for their appeal? Obviously, part of their popularity can be explained by their exciting adventures and larger-than-life personas, but could there be something deeper going on?

DC Comics was founded in the 1930s and effectively invented the superhero with the publication of *Action Comics* #1 in 1938. This issue introduced the iconic character of Superman, who would serve as an archetype (model) for countless future heroes. Batman was introduced soon afterward and was followed by Wonder Woman, the Flash, Green Lantern and many other classic characters. Most of these heroes were reimagined in the 1960s, establishing the template for their modern forms. The DC Universe (the fictional version of Earth which most DC characters occupy) has been "rebooted" several times in order to revise and streamline its characters' origins. This occurred in the 1980s (following the *Crisis on Infinite Earths* miniseries) and 2011 (after an event called Flashpoint). ⊗

Marvel Comics originated in 1939 as "Timely Publications" but was rebranded as "Marvel" in 1961. Creators including Stan Lee, Jack Kirby and Steve Ditko revolutionized the world of comics by introducing characters such as Spider-Man, the Avengers, the X-Men, and the Fantastic Four. In contrast to DC's heroes – two-dimensional do-gooders who mostly appealed to young readers – Marvel's characters were more conflicted and complicated. Its comics became popular on college campuses and often reflected real-world events. In contrast to the DC Universe, which features fictitious cities such as Metropolis and Gotham City, Marvel's stories are set in a world that more closely resembles our own. ⊗

Superman (DC, 1938). Kal-el was born to the scientist Jor-el and his wife Lara on the dying planet of Krypton. Unable to escape themselves before the planet was destroyed, the couple placed their infant son on a spaceship bound for the planet Earth. The ship landed in Kansas and was discovered by Jonathan and Martha Kent, a kindly couple who adopted the young alien and raised him as their own son. They named him Clark and soon learned that he possessed incredible abilities, which became more powerful as he got older. Clark eventually moved to the big city of Metropolis and became a reporter for the *Daily Planet* newspaper. Using his abilities to fight crime, he honored his Kryptonian heritage by wearing a costume emblazoned with the symbol of his family (which resembled the letter "S"). Another reporter at the *Planet*, Lois Lane, wrote a story about the mysterious hero that called him "Superman"; the name stuck. Superman has encountered an endless variety of threats, both on his adopted planet of Earth and throughout the galaxy. He is a founding member of the Justice League and has inspired many other heroes, including his cousin Kara – also a survivor of Krypton – who became known as Supergirl. Superman is extraordinarily powerful, possessing massive strength and virtual invulnerability along with the ability to fly, project "heat vision" out of his eyes, freeze objects with his breath, see through walls and move incredibly fast. He is vulnerable to magic and to remnants of his destroyed planet, which are composed of a material known as kryptonite. ⊗

The Justice League (DC, 1960). The Justice League (also called the Justice League of America, and spawning offshoots like Justice League Europe) is DC's premier superhero group. Although membership has varied over the years, it generally includes the DC Universe's most popular heroes: Superman, Batman, Wonder Woman, Green Lantern, the Flash, Aquaman, and the Martian Manhunter. (In recent years, Cyborg has been a frequent member as well.) The League is usually sanctioned and monitored by international authorities, although it also acts independently. It exists to deal with threats that are too great for any one hero to handle alone. ⊗

The Avengers (Marvel, 1963). The Avengers is Marvel's version of the Justice League: a super-group comprised of many of its most popular characters that addresses global threats. Its membership has changed dramatically over the years, but core characters include Thor, Captain America, Iron Man, Ant-Man, the Wasp, Hawkeye, the Black Widow, the Vision and the Scarlet Witch. Many other versions of the team have existed over the years, including the West Coast Avengers, the Great Lakes Avengers, the Young Avengers, and the Ultimate Avengers. ⊗

WHAT IS PHILOSOPHY? Philosophy has been defined in innumerable different ways. Philosophers like to philosophize about everything, including the nature of philosophy itself! For the purposes of this book, it can be described as a systematic attempt to think carefully and critically about fundamental concepts. Note that "thinking critically" doesn't necessarily mean criticizing something in a negative sense; instead, it refers to rational analysis that seeks to overcome biases and examine unstated assumptions. "Fundamental concepts" can be defined very broadly, including the deepest questions humans can ask. Why do we exist? What's the purpose of life? How do we know what we think we know? Ethics is a subset of philosophy that concerns questions of morality. This book is primarily focused on ethical issues but will also touch on other, related dimensions of philosophy. ❷ **How would you define** *philosophy*? **If you were asked to describe your personal philosophy, how would you respond? (Everybody has a philosophy — some of us have just thought about it more than others!)** φ

The Justice League of Ancient Greece. Socrates, Plato and Aristotle are the "founding fathers" of Western philosophy. They lived in the city-state of Athens during a time of great intellectual ferment and flourishing. Socrates (470 – 399 BCE) is only known through the writing of his students, the most prominent of whom is Plato (427 – 347 BCE). Plato composed a series of dialogues (discussions among different characters) that featured his teacher Socrates in conversation with other Athenians. It's difficult to know which ideas should be attributed to Socrates and which originated with Plato, but it's generally assumed that Plato's later works reflect his own positions. Neither philosopher developed a systematic theory of ethics, but both were concerned with concepts of justice, virtue, knowledge and truth. Aristotle (384 – 322 BCE) was a student of Plato's who argued that the purpose of human life is to achieve ethical and intellectual excellence. He developed an approach to ethics that regards "virtues" (dimensions of a good moral character) as a "golden mean" (happy medium) between unethical extremes. For example, the virtue of *courage* is midway between the "vices" of *cowardice* (the lack of courage) and *rashness* (an excessive and immoderate amount of courage). ϕ

ETHICAL REASONING. If someone gets into an "argument" in everyday life, this usually refers to a heated dispute that may or may not involve actual *reasons* for supporting one view over another. In philosophy, however, the term has a more specialized meaning. A person making a logical argument provides reasons and evidence to support a conclusion. For example, consider the claim "ethical reasoning is essential." The truth of this statement may seem obvious – especially to someone reading a book like this! – but what would you say to someone who doubted it? You could make an argument along these lines. Ethical questions are extraordinarily important because our views on moral issues (both as individuals and as a society) can help or harm other people. Although we all have ethical perspectives, we rarely think about them explicitly. Instead, we make decisions based on our "instincts" (a combination of our conscience, emotional reactions, and moral character), tradition (what we've been taught), assumptions (unexamined ideas we take for granted), biases (prejudices and other cognitive distortions), and peer pressure (humans have a powerful predisposition to go along with what our group thinks). Sometimes these factors lead us to the morally correct conclusion, but in other instances we end up behaving very badly. This is where ethical reasoning steps in to save the day. Logic enables us to avoid inconsistency, ethical principles provide goals and guidelines, and moral theories allow us to examine problems from different perspectives. Unfortunately, ethical reasoning is not like mathematics: except in the simplest of cases, it doesn't supply us with clear, unambiguous and irrefutable answers. It does, however, enable us to think more deeply about the moral values we hold and apply them to difficult ethical issues. Throughout the text, I'll be including advice on how to employ ethical reasoning and avoid common pitfalls that threaten to distort our thinking. These tips will be marked with this symbol: 🖼

WHAT ARE ETHICS? Part One: Obligations

At the most basic level, *ethics* are principles that enable us to determine what's right and wrong. They provide guidelines for how we ought to behave in our interactions with others. Ultimately, ethics derive from the relationships we have with other people (and, arguably, nonhuman animals). A situation involves ethical issues when our choices could help or harm someone else. In contrast, if a decision only affects *you* it's generally not considered ethical; you simply do what's in your own self-interest. (However, it could be argued that we have ethical obligations to ourselves.) For example, when a wealthy and self-centered playboy named Oliver Queen was marooned on a desert island that he initially believed to be uninhabited, his only concern was his own survival. Once he returned to civilization, he used the archery skills he had developed to become the superhero known as **Green Arrow**, fighting a war against crime on behalf of the disadvantaged and downtrodden. Queen's moral character had been transformed by his experience on the island. He abandoned his selfish pursuit of pleasure and devoted himself to helping others.

Green Arrow (DC, 1941). After returning from the island where he was marooned, Queen assumed a "Robin Hood" persona. He fights on behalf of the people of Star City, taking on corrupt corporations and politicians in addition to ordinary criminals and super-powered villains. Although Green Arrow has occasionally been part of the Justice League, he's usually more of a "street-level" hero who addresses down-to-earth problems instead of cosmic threats. ⊗

Familial Obligations

Our relationships with other people give rise to ethical *obligations* toward them. The specific obligations we have depend on the nature of the relationship. For example, *familial obligations* derive from relationships we're born into, involving parents and children, brothers and sisters, uncles and nieces, etc. What do parents owe their children? Although some general duties are obvious (food, shelter, safety, emotional support), specifics depend on the circumstances. For example, the scientist Jor-El and his wife Lara constructed a spaceship to save their infant son, Kal-El, from the dying planet of Krypton. Kal's adoptive earth parents, Jonathan and Martha Kent, had a very different set of obligations: they raised the young alien as their own child and instilled the moral values that enabled him to become Superman. Of course, parental obligations change as children age; as an adult, Clark Kent (Superman's alter ego) no longer needed his parents' help to get dressed or use the bathroom! Children also have obligations toward their parents, which likewise evolve as they get older. Superheroes can face unique challenges. Clark felt anguished when, despite his extraordinary abilities, he was unable to save his father from a fatal heart attack.

Personal Obligations

Personal obligations derive from relationships we choose: romantic relationships, friendships, etc. Like familial obligations, these are influenced by the society we inhabit and shaped by individual circumstances. Historically, husbands and wives had very different obligations toward one another, determined by societal expectations about how men and women ought to behave. Now, in "developed" (Westernized) countries like the U.S., these gender roles are less rigid and couples have more freedom to define their own relationships. These changes are reflected in the evolving portrayal of superhero characters. When the **Fantastic Four** were first introduced in the early 1960s, Sue Storm was called **The Invisible Girl** (her main power, tellingly, was to disappear!) and was subservient to her boyfriend and later husband, Reed Richards (aka **Mr. Fantastic**). Later, she changed her name to the more dignified **Invisible Woman** and was recognized as the most powerful member of the group: in addition to becoming invisible, Sue can create force fields. Still, she was largely responsible for raising the couple's children, Franklin and Valeria – which reflects the fact that women who work outside the home remain responsible for a disproportionate amount of childcare. Later in the series, in another sign of changing social norms, the preteen Valeria was recognized as her father's equal in terms of scientific genius. The Fantastic Four is unusual in being a family-based superhero group; friendships are far more common in crime-fighting teams. For example, **Luke Cage** (formerly called **Power Man**) and Danny Rand (**Iron Fist**) became close friends after becoming "Heroes for Hire." In general, obligations between friends are *symmetrical* (the same on both sides): our obligations to our friends are equivalent to their obligations to us. Again, however, circumstances can create differences: Luke was a wrongly convicted ex-con who was raised in poverty while Danny was the well-heeled heir to a multinational corporation. In other words, Iron Fist usually paid for lunch!

The Fantastic Four (Marvel, 1961). A brilliant scientist named Reed Richards was accompanied on a scientific expedition to outer space by his best friend Ben Grimm, his girlfriend Susan Storm, and Sue's brother Johnny. Bombarded by cosmic radiation during the voyage, upon returning to Earth they discovered that they possessed amazing abilities. Reed, who could stretch his body to incredible lengths and was virtually impervious to harm, became known as Mr. Fantastic; Susan could turn invisible and create powerful force fields; Johnny (aka the Human Torch) could generate and project flame, which also enabled him to fly; and Ben was transformed into the Thing, a "monster" covered in orange, rock-like scales who was tremendously strong and resistant to harm. Although the Fantastic Four use their powers to defend the innocent and protect the Earth from alien threats, they also see themselves as scientists and explorers in search of new civilizations and ideas. They are a family first and foremost, and are celebrities in the Marvel Universe because their identities are publicly known. ⊗

Luke Cage and Iron Fist (Marvel, 1972 and 1974). Wrongly convicted of a crime he didn't commit, Carl Lucas volunteered for an experimental procedure in prison. It granted him superhuman strength and invulnerability, and after being released Lucas – who now called himself "Luke Cage" – used his powers to become a "Hero for Hire." Unlike Luke, Daniel Rand was born into a wealthy and powerful family. As a young boy he accompanied his parents on an expedition to the sacred city of K'un-L'un. After his parents were killed, Danny trained with the warrior monks of K'un-L'un and ultimately defeated a mystical dragon known as Shou-Lao. He became the Iron Fist, capable of using his *chi* (life energy) to enhance his physical strength and to heal himself or others. After returning to

New York City, Rand became business partners and best friends with Luke Cage. In addition to helping people (for the right price) as the Heroes for Hire, Luke and Danny have been members of both the Avengers and the Defenders. The latter team also includes Luke's wife, the superhero/detective Jessica Jones. ⊗

Legal Obligations

Legal obligations derive from the laws of the city, state and country in which we live, including legally binding contracts. This is a good place to point out that moral obligations can fall into more than one category at the same time. For example, the parental obligation to care for your children and keep them safe is also a legal obligation; the authorities can remove your children if you abuse or neglect them. (In one story arc, Franklin and Valeria Richards were taken from their parents because Child Protective Services determined that the Baxter Building — the Fantastic Four's headquarters, which was frequently attacked by the team's enemies — was an unsafe environment.) In general, superheroes have a complicated relationship with the law. Some groups (like the Avengers and the Justice League) are officially sanctioned by the government and have the legal authority to protect the world from global threats. Most heroes, however, are vigilantes: they operate outside the law and are sometimes pursued by the police (or other heroes) themselves. For example, the **Punisher** has waged a one-man war on crime since criminals murdered his family. Unlike most heroes, he uses guns and kills his enemies instead of tying (or webbing) them up and leaving them for the authorities. Over in Gotham City, Batman occupies a kind of legal gray zone: he's not officially authorized to fight crime but regularly collaborates with the police commissioner, Jim Gordon. Both Batman and the Punisher are convinced (based on tragic personal experience) that the law often fails to protect innocents and therefore believe they are entitled to break the law in pursuit of justice.

ETHICS AND THE LAW. Ethics and the law are closely connected. Most legal rules — the prohibition of murder, to cite an obvious example — derive from our society's consensus that unjustified killing is morally wrong. However, ethics and the law are distinct from each other in important ways. In general, laws prevent us from *harming* others; they rarely require us to actively *help* other people. (So-called "Good Samaritan" laws are very rare, although they do sometimes apply in emergencies to individuals with medical training.) In addition, ethical principles can compel us to violate laws that we regard as unjust. The Civil Rights Movement was motivated by the belief that laws which mandate racial segregation are wrong. Ultimately, court decisions like *Brown v. Board of Education* (1954) and legislation including the Civil Rights Act (1964) and Voting Rights Act (1965) vindicated the views of Martin Luther King, Jr. and other activists, outlawing explicit discrimination. ϕ

❷ Should the law always be followed or are individuals justified in violating laws that they think are wrong? If the latter, is there a danger that laws will be broken for self-serving (selfish) reasons instead of morally principled reasons? Thinking about today's society, are there any laws that you regard as unjust?

Dietrich Bonhoeffer (1906 - 1945) was a German pastor and theologian who vocally opposed the Nazi regime. He helped found the Confessing Church, a dissident group of German Christians who refused to collaborate with the Nazis. Bonhoeffer left for the U.S. in 1939 and could have remained there in safety until the war ended, but he felt obligated to return to Germany. Despite serious moral reservations, he participated in a failed plot to assassinate Hitler and was imprisoned in 1943. Bonhoeffer was executed in 1945 just weeks before Allied forces liberated Berlin. He left behind a rich legacy of theological and ethical writings, some of which were composed while he was in prison. In his view, Christians are obligated to emulate Jesus Christ, a "suffering God" who opposed evil and injustice in the world. Bonhoeffer had no interest in abstract, theoretical ethics: he advocated a form of Virtue Ethics which acknowledges that moral dilemmas are unavoidable in real life. Instead of seeking a perfect solution and trying to remain "morally pure," Christians are called to *act* (even in the face of uncertainty) by following the self-sacrificial example of Jesus. *Bonhoeffer's superpower: outstanding integrity, living (and dying) in accordance with his moral values.* ϕ

The Punisher (Marvel, 1974). After his wife and children were murdered by the mob for witnessing a crime, Frank Castle declared a one-man war on criminals. Calling himself the Punisher, Castle used his military training to become a homicidal vigilante. Unlike most superheroes in the Marvel Universe, the Punisher kills his targets and will use torture to extract information when necessary. He believes that criminals deserve to die and does not trust the law enforcement system to carry out justice. Castle is often opposed by other heroes, who condemn his vindictive perspective and brutal methods. Although the Punisher lacks superhuman abilities, he is a highly skilled marksman and combatant who has access to numerous weapons and other technologies. ⊗

Professional Obligations

Professional obligations derive from our occupation. Employees have obligations to their employers (and to their fellow employees), as do bosses to their workers. The blind hero known as **Daredevil** is also Matthew Murdock, a practicing lawyer. Although he breaks the law (Daredevil is a vigilante) when fighting crime in the guise of his acrobatic alter ego, he upholds it when defending his clients. Murdock has legally-defined obligations toward the people who hire him, including the duty of confidentiality (keeping secrets). Similarly, both Clark Kent (Superman) and his sometimes girlfriend/wife Lois Lane work as journalists. As reporters, they are bound by a code of ethics to tell the truth, protect their sources, etc. Of course, Clark's *other* job (being the Man of Steel) also includes certain professional obligations, and *these* obligations (to save people's lives and defeat super-villians) often conflict with his journalistic duties. Consequently, Clark routinely faces moral dilemmas: should he finish the story he's working on or save Metropolis from an alien invasion? When our obligations conflict, we're forced to decide which ones take precedence. (Fortunately, Clark is able to think and type at super-speed so he can usually save the world *and* meet his deadline.)

Great Responsibility

> **Daredevil** (Marvel, 1964).   As a young boy, Matt Murdock was blinded by radioactive waste, which enhanced his other senses and endowed him with a superhuman "radar sense." His father, a boxer named Jack Murdock, was killed by the mob after refusing to throw a fight.   The younger Murdock became Daredevil, bringing his father's killers to justice and fighting crime in the Hell's Kitchen neighborhood of New York City. Murdock also earned a law degree and, along with his fellow superhero-lawyer Jennifer Walters (aka She-Hulk), frequently represents other superheroes in legal matters. Although Daredevil is blind, his senses of hearing, smell, touch and taste are greatly enhanced. He also possesses a radar sense that provides him with a 360-degree perspective on his surroundings. In addition, Daredevil is an accomplished acrobat and a highly skilled fighter who is trained in multiple forms of martial arts.   He uses specially-designed billy clubs as weapons. ⊗

What *professional obligations* do superheroes have? Most superheroes are independently-operating vigilantes who don't get paid or answer to a boss. Still, being a hero is definitely a vocation, and heroes are bound by a set of obligations once they decide to fight for truth and justice. First and foremost, they should protect innocent lives. That's the top priority for nearly every hero, even ones (like the Punisher) who are convinced that the guilty deserve to die. Equally important, however, is defeating super villains — in part because their nefarious plans often threaten to kill hundreds if not thousands of people. In some cases, however, the duty to defeat villains may conflict with the duty to protect innocents: when super humans fight titanic battles in the middle of a crowded city, "collateral damage" (a euphemism for noncombatants who get caught in the crossfire) is inevitable. That's why responsible heroes try to relocate fights to less populated areas whenever possible. Villains often exploit this "weakness" by intentionally placing civilians in harm's way to distract their opponents — especially when they're facing exceptionally powerful heroes (like Superman) whom they could never hope to defeat in a fair fight. Superheroes are also obligated to minimize the damage their conflicts cause to property. Although this obligation is far less important than the duty to protect people's lives — as evidenced by the fact that heroes routinely throw cars at their enemies and punch them into buildings — it's not insignificant.

Superhuman battles surely cause hundreds of millions of dollars of damage every year in the DC and Marvel Universes, and the cost of insurance to cover this kind of loss must be astronomical! This is another advantage villains have over heroes: they rarely care about the damage they cause. Yet another disparity: heroes have obligations toward villains themselves that the villains are very unlikely to reciprocate. With the exception of homicidal heroes who intentionally kill their enemies, superheroes should only use enough force to incapacitate their foes without causing permanent harm. This must be especially difficult when they're fighting villains (or the hired minions of villains) who lack superpowers: there's a fine line between rendering someone unconscious and causing paralysis or permanent brain damage. Perhaps superheroes themselves have to purchase insurance policies (at least ones whose real identities are publicly known). It's easy to imagine heroes getting sued by criminals for using excessive force and causing emotional distress. (Fighting Batman in a dark alley could very easily result in post-traumatic stress disorder!) In summary, the morality of being a superhero is very complicated – heroes are forced to make split-second decisions that balance a complex set of conflicting obligations. No wonder so many super humans turn to villainy! It's much simpler, and you can actually get paid. In the long term, of course, crime *doesn't* pay, because heroes almost always win in the end.

❓ Do you see any parallels between the professional obligations of superheroes and those of real-life police officers? What kind of moral conflicts do the police confront?

Humanitarian Obligations

Humanitarian obligations are more abstract. Instead of deriving from specific relationships to people we know, they involve obligations to help people in need who are strangers to us. Unlike familial, personal and professional obligations, our duty to humanity doesn't require reciprocity: we help others because we *can* and have no expectation of being helped in return. Although superheroes often save their loved ones (how many times has Lois Lane fallen from a tall building?), in general they're motivated by humanitarian impulses. Remember Uncle Ben's maxim: "with great power comes great responsibility." The greater our ability to help people in need, the stronger our obligation to do so. This obviously applies to incredibly powerful heroes like Superman and **Dr. Strange** (Earth's Sorcerer Supreme, who protects our dimension from magical threats), but also motivates "ordinary" heroes (who lack superhuman powers) like Batman and Green Arrow. Like us, superheroes face the difficult question of how far their humanitarian obligations extend. Arguably, heroes like Superman should spend *all* their time saving people in need. Every moment he spends romancing Lois Lane or hanging out with Jimmy Olsen translates into people dying: somewhere around the world there are disasters he could be averting. Although his life as Clark Kent may keep him grounded and sane, it comes at a heavy price! Likewise, we ordinary humans can and should ask how much we are obligated to give. Even if you're not wealthy by American standards, if you live in the Western world you're likely to be vastly better off than most people living in developing countries. All the money you spend on yourself, your family and your friends for things you don't actually need could do an *enormous* amount of good for the world's poor, many of whom are chronically malnourished and lack access to even basic sanitation and health care. Instead of buying a new car, you could save dozens of people's lives. Should you?

Dr. Strange (Marvel, 1963). Stephen Strange was a brilliant but arrogant surgeon who was badly injured in a car accident. When modern medicine proved incapable of restoring the use of his hands, Strange sought answers in the world of magic. He ended up as the disciple of the Ancient One, an immensely powerful wizard living deep in the Himalaya Mountains. After the Ancient One's physical body was killed in battle with an extra-dimensional threat, Dr. Strange took his place as the Sorcerer Supreme of the Marvel Universe. Strange is a highly skilled sorcerer with an encyclopedic knowledge of spells. He also possesses a variety of powerful mystical artifacts, including the Cloak of Levitation and the Eye of Agamotto. ⊗

Peter Singer (1946 – present). Singer is an Australian philosopher who specializes in applied ethics. He's best known for his contributions to debates about animal rights, bioethics, and the obligations of Western countries to the global poor. As a Utilitarian, Singer argues that we should make moral choices that maximize the well-being of all sentient beings who are affected by our decisions. This includes nonhuman animals, who are not "equal" to humans in every sense but have the same desire to avoid pain. In his view, eating meat is not generally justified since the suffering inflicted on food animals outweighs the pleasure that humans get from consuming them. In addition, Singer argues that most Americans (and citizens of other wealthy countries) should devote more of their income to help desperately poor people in developing countries. By sacrificing unnecessary luxuries, we could provide them with life-saving food, medicine, etc. *Superpower: Making his readers feel guilty for their moral failings – and motivating many of them to do more to help.* ϕ

REASONING VS. RATIONALIZING. When we engage in ethical *reasoning*, we apply ethical principles to moral problems using logic and evidence. All too often, however, we're guilty of *rationalizing* when we think we're reasoning. Instead of striving to be impartial (unbiased) and following our trail of thought wherever it leads, we *start* with our preferred conclusion and come up with arguments to support that point of view. For example, we might respond to the claim that we should give more of our income to help people living in desperate poverty by insisting (falsely) that all the money given to charities is wasted. Although it's true that *some* charities are inefficient and ineffective, pay their CEOs excessively high salaries, etc., that's clearly not true of *all* charities. As websites like Charity Navigator and The Life You Can Save reveal, many organizations will put your money to work and provide help where it's desperately needed. There may be other, valid reasons why we aren't obligated to be more generous, but it's intellectually dishonest to rely on false claims in support of our views. ▣

▣ **Think of a strong opinion you hold that you haven't thought about very deeply (perhaps because it's never been challenged). How would you respond if you were asked to come up with reasons to support your view? If you couldn't come up with any valid reasons, would you be tempted to rationalize?**

SUPEREROGATORY ACTIONS. An action is *supererogatory* if it goes above and beyond what our duty requires. While we're morally *required* to fulfill our obligations, we can *choose* to do more than is expected of us. For example, giving to charity or volunteering for a worthy cause is usually considered supererogatory. However, this depends on how one understands humanitarian obligations. Some philosophers argue that we are *obligated* to assist those who are less fortunate than us if we have the capacity to do so: in other words, "with great power comes great responsibility." φ

❓ **What do you think? If we have a duty to help strangers, how far does that duty extend?**

MORAL SAINTS AND PSYCHOPATHS. Some people have an extraordinarily powerful *conscience*, the internal sense of right and wrong that causes us to feel guilty if we fail to fulfill our moral obligations. Philosophers call them "moral saints" or "extreme altruists." (*Altruism* is self-sacrificial behavior on behalf of other people, i.e. the opposite of selfishness.) Convinced that they have the same duty to strangers as ordinary people have to their friends and family members, these individuals feel compelled to make extreme sacrifices to help those in need. At the other end of the ethical spectrum, *psychopaths* have a very weak or nonexistent conscience. Although they can rationally recognize the difference between right and wrong, they feel no guilt when they violate moral rules and harm other people. Many (but not all) superheroes are extreme altruists, feeling driven to help everyone they can and suffering great guilt when they inevitably fail. They often sacrifice their own, personal happiness in pursuit of justice. In a recent Batman story arc, Bruce Wayne's longtime love interest Selina Kyle (aka **Catwoman**) broke off their engagement to be married when she realized that Bruce could no longer be Batman if he was happy. In contrast, many super villains are psychopaths. The **Joker** provides an extreme example: he wants to create chaos and is willing to terrorize and murder hundreds of innocent people to achieve this end. φ

❓ **Do you know any moral saints or psychopaths in real life (or people with tendencies toward those character traits)? What do you think motivates them? Do they seem happy? Are they difficult for "ordinary" people to deal with and understand?**

Catwoman (DC, 1940). Selina Kyle was a high-end cat burglar whose crimes were often foiled by Batman. Over time Catwoman and Batman developed an attraction for one another, and at different times in the characters' histories they've been romantically involved. (In a recent story arc Kyle and Bruce Wayne were engaged to be married.) Although she originated as a villain, over time Catwoman became a reluctant and ambivalent hero. She still has a taste for the finer things in life and will readily steal what she wants, but she usually makes the right decision when innocent lives are at stake. Catwoman lacks superhuman abilities but is an expert thief and a skilled martial artist. ⊗

The Joker (DC, 1940). The Joker's origins are shrouded in mystery, in part because the character has told different stories about his background with contradictory details. The one commonality is that he fell into a vat of chemical waste, turning his skin pale white and his hair green. As he's usually depicted, the Joker is a dangerous and unpredictable psychopath with a twisted sense of humor. (Some versions of the character have portrayed him as a mischievous but ultimately harmless trickster.) He thrives on chaos and is utterly obsessed with Batman. The Joker is responsible for the deaths of hundreds if not thousands of innocent people, many of whom he's murdered in cruel, shocking and sadistic ways. Although he doesn't possess super powers, he's a scientific genius: in addition to inventing Joker venom, which causes its victims to erupt in spasms of ultimately lethal laughter, he's capable of constructing fiendishly complicated death traps. ⊗

Civic Obligations

Civic obligations derive from the relationship between individuals and the communities in which they live. In most societies this involves the government: we're obligated to follow the law, pay our taxes, and be loyal citizens. In return, the government is generally expected to provide stability, security, protection from violence, infrastructure (e.g. roads and bridges), and the necessities of life (food, shelter, health care). Depending on their political perspective, people differ about how far they think the government's duties extend. Libertarians, for example, usually argue that help for the needy ought to come mostly if not exclusively from private charities fulfilling their humanitarian obligations; they oppose the use of taxpayer money to provide assistance. Socialists, in contrast, have a far more expansive view of the government's role, arguing that it should guarantee full access to housing, education, health care, etc. to its citizens. In the comic-book universes, superheroes exist (in part) because state and national governments are incapable of adequately protecting their citizens. Although both DC and Marvel feature government-run super-teams (the **Suicide Squad** and the **Thunderbolts**, both of which consist of partially-reformed villains), they aren't capable of fully protecting the populace. Between alien invasions, villainous schemes, and massively destructive super battles, cities (and sometimes entire countries) are nearly destroyed on a regular basis. Some characters (like the Black Panther, king of the fictional African nation of Wakanda and Dr. Doom, dictator of Latveria) rule their own nations, which forces them to balance their royal (or authoritarian) duties with their heroic (or villainous) activities.

STRAW MAN AND STEEL MAN ARGUMENTS. A person commits the "straw man" fallacy when she misrepresents the perspective she's arguing against, making it seem far weaker and less plausible than the position her opponents actually hold. For example, a socialist may accuse a libertarian of being a selfish psychopath who doesn't care if his fellow citizens starve in the streets. This may accurately describe an extreme fringe of people who hold libertarian views, but it clearly isn't the mainstream view among libertarians! (Conversely, a libertarian could falsely claim that socialists want to confiscate money from the rich in order to make everyone equally poor.) Although the temptation to engage in this form of argumentation is understandable – it's much easier to "win" an argument against an absurd and unconvincing caricature of an opposing perspective – this approach is both intellectually unfair and strategically counter-productive. The straw man fallacy is a form of cheating; it may help you "win" an argument in the short-term but is likely to backfire in the long-term. You'll lose credibility when the people you persuaded realize that you misrepresented the opposing position. Instead of creating and easily defeating a straw man, you should construct a "steel man":

the most plausible version of the perspective you're arguing against. If you can legitimately overcome the *strongest* objections your opponent could devise, you can be confident that you're presenting the best and most compelling version of your own position. Moreover, constructing a "steel man" can increase your appreciation for opposing points of view, leading you to modify your argument by incorporating their insights. At the very least, you'll be able to better understand (and respect) your opponents. 📖

❓ **Think of a moral position that you oppose, then come up with both "straw man" and "steel man" versions of an argument which someone who holds that position might make. Do the same for your own perspective on the issue.**

LOGICAL FALLACIES. A logical fallacy is an error in the logical form of an argument. In "formal" logical arguments, the conclusion of an argument that commits a fallacy *cannot* be true. However, the fallacies discussed in this text are of the "informal" variety. If you spot a fallacy in an "informal" (less technical) argument there's no *guarantee* that the conclusion is false. However, the presence of fallacy gives you reason to suspect that the argument is weak and that its conclusion may be untrue. 📖

The Suicide Squad (DC, 1987). Created and directed by a ruthless government official named Amanda Waller, the Suicide Squad consists of captured super-villains who agree to undertake dangerous missions in exchange for time off their prison sentences. Most members of the Squad have tiny explosives implanted in their brains to guarantee their loyalty; if they try to escape or go "off mission" in any way, Waller can detonate the devices. In contrast to conventional superheroes, the Squad uses violent and often illegal methods to complete their missions. Although the roster of members has varied over the years, it usually includes Captain Boomerang (a Flash rogue who mostly provides comic relief), Deadshot (an unerring assassin), Enchantress (a megalomaniacal sorceress), Killer Croc (a brutal Batman villain), and Harley Quinn (a former sidekick to the Joker who is also insane). ⊗

> **The Thunderbolts** (Marvel, 1997). Like the Suicide Squad, the Thunderbolts is a team comprised of former villains who posed as heroes; ultimately, they came under the supervision of the U.S. government. ⊗

Religious Obligations

Religious obligations, finally, derive from one's religious beliefs. Believers have obligations to their God – or gods – as well as obligations to their fellow believers and, more broadly, humanity itself (religious obligations often inspire humanitarian duties). Religion occupies a complicated space in the world of superheroes. It's often ignored altogether; with a few exceptions (for example, Daredevil and the **X-Men's Nightcrawler** are devout Catholics), the religious identity of heroes is rarely mentioned. In recent years, both Marvel and DC have diversified their fictional worlds by introducing prominent Muslim characters (respectively: Kamala Khan, the new **Ms. Marvel**, and a Green Lantern named Simon Baz), but overall religion remains marginal to most heroes. Interestingly, both companies include deities from Greco-Roman mythology (Wonder Woman was granted her powers by the Greek gods; Hercules has often been a member of the Avengers) and Marvel has delved deeply into Norse myth. In general, however, the gods and goddesses of comic books are not objects of worship; they're presented as extraordinarily powerful and long-lived beings who were mistaken for "gods" in the distant past.

> **The X-Men** (Marvel, 1963). The X-Men are a team of mutants (individuals born with genetic mutations which grant them strange abilities) assembled by Professor Charles Xavier, an enormously powerful telepath who is a mutant himself. Xavier envisions a world in which mutants and humans can live together in peace. Xavier is opposed by his former friend and archrival Magneto, who is convinced that humans will always fear, distrust and persecute mutants. The X-Men originally consisted of five teenage mutants named Cyclops, Iceman, the Beast, Angel, and Marvel Girl; its membership was later expanded to include dozens of different

mutant heroes on a variety of different teams. Prominent X-Men include Storm, Wolverine, Colossus, Kitty Pryde (aka Shadowcat), Gambit, Rogue and Psylocke. ⊗

Nightcrawler (Marvel, 1975). Kurt Wagner is a German-born mutant with the ability to teleport himself and others short distances. Unlike most mutants, whose mutations only manifest themselves once they reach puberty, Wagner's mutation was obvious from birth. He's covered in short blue fur and has a "demonic" appearance, with pointed ears, glowing eyes and a forked tale. Abandoned by his mother (who was later revealed to be the shape-shifting villain Mystique) at an early age, he was raised in the circus and worked as an acrobat until Professor Xavier recruited him. Nightcrawler is a devout Catholic. In one story arc, Wagner died and ascended to Heaven, but voluntarily left paradise and returned to Earth when his friends needed him. ⊗

Ms. Marvel (Marvel, 2013). Inspired by the original Ms. Marvel, an Avenger who later adopted the name Captain Marvel, Kamala Khan decided to become a superhero when exposure to the "Terrigen Mists" activated her latent Inhuman powers. Ms. Marvel can enlarge, shrink and stretch different parts of her body and is mostly impervious to harm. Her parents emigrated to the U.S. from Pakistan; Khan herself is a practicing Muslim. ⊗

THE PROBLEM OF EVIL. Does God have obligations toward *us?* According to some believers, the question itself is blasphemous because God is our Creator and owes us nothing. Philosophers, however, have posed the following dilemma: if God is all-powerful (as Christians, Muslims and Jews believe) and loves us, why is there so much unnecessary suffering in the world? Believers have offered numerous responses. Perhaps our suffering only *seems* unnecessary but actually serves a purpose we can't understand; maybe people who experience suffering are being justly punished by God; much of the suffering in the world is caused by people who are abusing their free will, not God. However, even many believers admit that none of these explanations is fully satisfying. The apparent silence of God in the face of horrendous human suffering poses a profound challenge to believers who seek solace in their faith. In one story arc in the Marvel Universe, a growing movement of people began worshiping **Thor,** the Norse god of Thunder. In contrast to the transcendent and hidden God of Christianity, Thor (a founding member of the Avengers) is highly visible and helps people in unmistakable ways. In a more recent story, an alien named Gorr vowed vengeance against all "gods" when the so-called deities of his society failed to save his family. Gorr (the "God Butcher") murdered hundreds of gods from different planets until Thor finally stopped him. ϕ

❓ Do you think God has moral obligations toward God's creation? Why or why not? If you don't believe in God, is the Problem of Evil part of the reason why? Presumably any of us would prevent a terrible tragedy (e.g., a mass shooting or devastating earthquake) if we had the power to do so, yet God (if God exists) does not. Are we, in some sense, more ethical than God? Is it possible that God transcends our limited human ideas of right and wrong?

Thor (Marvel, 1962). Thor is the Norse god of thunder, an immensely powerful and long-lived being who was worshiped as a deity by the ancient Vikings. In addition to his great strength and ability to summon lightning, Thor wields an enchanted hammer known as Mjolnir that enables him to fly, deflect attacks, and transport himself through space. (In a recent story arc Thor lost his moral "worthiness" and was no longer able to lift Mjolnir; he was temporarily replaced by the human Jane Foster, who was transformed by the hammer into a female version of the thunder god.) Thor is often called to defend the mystical realm of Asgard alongside other Norse gods, including his father Odin and his mother Freya. He is occasionally assisted (but more often manipulated and opposed) by his mischievous half-brother Loki, an untrustworthy trickster god. Thor has often been a member of the Avengers, defending Midgard (the Asgardian name for Earth) alongside his human teammates. ⊗

To summarize: ethics are based on obligations that we have toward other people that derive from our relationships with them. Some of these duties (*familial, personal,* and *professional*) apply to individuals we actually know, while others (*humanitarian, societal* and *religious*) oblige us in a more abstract sense. *Legal obligations* can be based on either direct relationships or impersonal laws, and – like all other obligations – can fall into more than one category at once. In most cases fulfillment of our obligations is simple and straightforward. If you're a parent you should love and support your child; if you're an employee, you should show up for work on time and perform your job properly. However, what if one half of a relationship violates their obligations? In one Avengers story line, Hank Pym (the original **Ant-Man**) was physically and emotionally abusive to his wife Janet Van Dyne (the original **Wasp**). Obviously, that alters her obligations toward him! In still other cases, there's disagreement about what our obligations actually are. These disputes can derive from different political views (what does society owe us, and what do we owe society?), divergent ideas about what relationships require (what roles should a husband and wife play in a marriage?), or differences in our *moral values*.

? **What moral obligations are most important to you? Are there instances in which you've failed to fulfill your obligations to others, or times in your life when other people have failed you? How did you (or they) respond? Do these failures reflect badly on your (their) moral character, or were they caused by unavoidable circumstances? How do you respond when your moral obligations conflict with one another? Try to think of an example when this occurred and describe how the conflict was resolved.**

Ant-Man and the Wasp (Marvel, 1963). The original Ant-Man and the Wasp were founding members of the Avengers alongside Thor, the Hulk and Iron Man. Hank Pym was a brilliant scientist who discovered what came to be called Pym Particles, subatomic particles that can increase and decrease the size of objects. Pym could also use the particles to greatly increase his size and strength, becoming Giant-Man (aka Goliath). In addition, he invented a helmet that enabled him to communicate with insects, which he used to become the miniature superhero known as Ant-Man. (The current Ant-Man is an ex-con named Scott Lang who stole Pym's Ant-Man suit to save his daughter Cassie.) Janet Van Dyne was the daughter of a wealthy scientist who was killed as a result of one of his experiments; she asked Pym for help in avenging his death. He imbued her body with Pym particles, which enabled her to shrink, grow wings and project bio-electrical blasts. Pym and Van Dyne have been romantically involved for much of the characters' history. ⊗

WHAT ARE ETHICS? Part Two: Moral Values

Moral values are ethical ideals (principles) or standards of behavior that we strive to uphold. Every individual has his or her own set of ideals, but some values are widely held across society. Others only apply to specific communities within the broader culture. *Values* are closely related to *virtues* (ingrained habits which predispose us to act in accordance with values we hold) and *vices* (the predisposition to violate our community's values). In other words, values are intimately connected to our moral character: whether we're a "good guy" or "bad guy." Of course, very few of us are completely good (morally virtuous) or bad (morally vicious). Most of us fall somewhere in between and struggle to live in accordance with our values. The same is true of the most interesting and compelling comic-book characters. Heroes who are unquestionably good (like Superman, a paragon of virtue who only "breaks bad" when he's corrupted by magic or exposed to red kryptonite) and villains who are irredeemably evil (like the villain Doomsday, a force of destruction who once succeeded in killing Superman) have their place. However, "anti-heroes" (heroes who use vicious tactics and sometimes veer into villainy, like the Punisher and **Wolverine**) are often more interesting, as are villains who have more complicated motivations and sometimes fight for good (e.g., the X-Men's sometimes foe and sometimes ally **Magneto**). Imperfect heroes and ambivalent villains are more realistic and compelling because they resemble actual humans, who have a mixture of good and bad traits and don't automatically do the right (or wrong) thing. Like comic books, morality is rarely just black and white.

Wolverine (Marvel, 1974). John Howlett (later called "Logan") was a mutant born in the 1880s; his power to heal from almost any injury makes him almost immortal. He enlisted in the Canadian military to fight in World War I and served with Captain America during World War II. He was later subjected to medical experiments by the government's Weapon X program, which took advantage of his healing ability to bond adamantium (a fictitious and virtually unbreakable metal) to his bones. After escaping from his captors, he was recruited by Charles Xavier to become a member of the X-Men. Logan's mutant ability enables him to recover from almost any injury; he also possesses extraordinarily acute senses, especially his sense of smell. Wolverine has retractable claws that emerge on command from each of his hands — like the rest of his bones, they're coated with adamantium. An older version of Logan from an alternate reality (called "Old Man Logan") also exists in the Marvel Universe, as does a female clone of Wolverine who's known as X-23. ⊗

Magneto (Marvel, 1963). Born to a Jewish family in 1920s Germany, the man who became Magneto lost his family in the Holocaust and only escaped Auschwitz himself due the manifestation of his mutant powers. (Like Wolverine, he ages very slowly.) He adopted the name "Magnus" and married a woman named Magda after the war; the couple's daughter was killed by a mob after they discovered his abilities. Calling himself Eric Lehnsherr, Magneto met and befriended a fellow mutant named Charles Xavier. Lehnsherr came to believe that Xavier and his X-Men were hopelessly naive: humans would never accept mutants as their equals, but would always fear, distrust and persecute them. Magneto formed the Brotherhood of Evil Mutants to pursue his goal of mutant domination. Magneto's philosophy has evolved over the years. (At one point he even led the X-Men in Xavier's absence.) Still, he remains deeply suspicious of humankind and is fiercely dedicated to the protection of mutants. Magneto possesses the ability to manipulate magnetic fields, enabling him to control all forms of metal. ⊗

VIRTUE ETHICS. Virtue Ethics is an approach to morality that emphasizes moral *character* rather than the rightness or wrongness of specific actions. Instead of asking "Should I do this or not?" in a particular circumstance, it focuses on becoming a good person by achieving moral excellence. People are considered *virtuous* if they possess character traits (like courage, compassion, honesty, etc.) that predispose them to do the right thing when confronted with moral challenges. In contrast, people are *vicious* if they have depraved moral habits (like cowardice, cruelty, and dishonesty) that cause them to behave badly by default. According to Virtue Ethics, the goal of the ethical life is to replace your vices with virtues, which is unfortunately easier to say than to do! Like other kinds of character traits, moral habits can become deeply ingrained, requiring dedication and repetition to completely change. For most of us, then, goodness remains a goal we are imperfectly striving toward rather than a destination we can ever reach. ϕ

> ❓ **What virtues do you possess? Do you have any vices? If so, have you ever tried to break these bad moral habits, and were you successful?**

      In the real world, very few of us are perfectly virtuous or completely vicious. We don't always and automatically do the right (or wrong) thing when confronted with a moral choice; we struggle. Comic book characters can illustrate this internal conflict in unique and evocative ways. For example, **Venom** is an enemy (and sometimes ally) of Spider-Man who is physically and psychologically bonded with an alien creature known as a symbiote. Although the symbiote has its own consciousness and can influence its host, its morality is shaped by the character of the human to whom it's bonded. The symbiote who became Venom was originally conjoined to Spider-Man, who found himself becoming more ruthless and violent under its influence. After Peter Parker rid himself of the symbiote, it bonded with an embittered reporter named Eddie Brock who wrongly blamed Spider-Man for his professional failures. Brock eventually abandoned his vendetta against Spider-Man and become a vigilante hero in his own right. Later, the symbiote became connected to an outright villain (Mac Gargan, formerly known as the Scorpion) and, later still, a bona fide hero (Flash Thompson, an army veteran and a good friend of Parker's), each time reflecting the vices and virtues of its host. This seems like an apt metaphor for the moral life. Even when we know, intellectually, how we ought to behave, an inner voice may lead us astray. According to some religious teachings, these temptations derive from demonic forces. In naturalistic (scientific) terms, they reflect aspects of our upbringing and the hard realities of human nature. Regardless, our moral values can stand against these self-serving inclinations and inspire us to live ethically, however difficult that might be.

> **Venom** (Marvel, 1984/1988). The symbiote first appeared in the *Secret Wars* miniseries as a black-and-white costume Spider-Man obtained on an alien planet. The Eddie Brock version of Venom made his debut four years later and was followed by many other variations on the character (including "offspring" of Venom like Carnage, a symbiote who bonded with a psychopathic serial killer). The symbiote grants its host superhuman strength, speed, agility and resistance to injury, and can shift its shape to increase Venom's size,

immobilize opponents, create weapons, generate weblines (similar to Spider-Man's), etc. Venom is vulnerable to fire and sonic attacks. ⊗

INTELLECTUAL VIRTUES AND VICES. *Moral* virtues and vices are character traits that lead us to act ethically or unethically. Likewise, *intellectual* virtues and vices predispose us to think well or poorly. Unsurprisingly, these positive and negative mental habits are mirror opposites of one another. Careful and critical thinkers are humble: they acknowledge that they might to wrong and remain open to learning from others. In contrast, careless thinkers are arrogant, assuming that they "know it all" and unwilling to engage in genuine dialogue with anyone who has an opposing view. Intellectually virtuous individuals strive for objectivity: insofar as possible (and it's never *completely* possible), they pursue the truth without being unduly influenced by their own feelings, desires and opinions. Conversely, bad thinking is distorted by biases, prejudices, and unexamined assumptions. Along the same lines, critical thinkers are fair-minded: they try to understand other people's perspectives openly, impartially and in the best possible light. Their intellectual opposites are close-minded, refusing to fairly consider other points of view and misrepresenting the positions of their opponents. Such people are also prone to stubbornness, refusing to rethink and revise their perspective regardless of the evidence and arguments against it. The virtuous, finally, are intellectually adaptable, willing to admit they were wrong and change their mind when the situation warrants it. 🖼

❓On balance, do you think you're more virtuous or vicious in an intellectual sense? Does it depend on the topic being discussed? – i.e., are you less open-minded about some issues than others

Justice

Justice is a central value in almost every society. In the simplest terms, it means giving people what they're due, which can be either positive (payment or some other reward) or negative (punishment). If J. Jonah Jameson (the publisher of the *Daily Bugle* newspaper) refused to pay freelance photographer Peter Parker what he was promised for his latest batch of Spider-Man pictures, that would be unjust and Peter would be rightfully upset. Fortunately, Peter usually gets paid. Jameson has many other moral vices — he's impatient and intolerant and stubbornly refuses to admit that Spider-Man is a hero rather than a menace — but he eventually pays Peter what he's owed. Conversely, if Spider-Man catches the Rhino (or one of his many other villains) robbing a bank, that criminal deserves to be punished for his crime. According to the principle of *proportionality*, the punishment should fit the crime: more serious crimes deserve harsher penalties. Of course, some heroes have different ideas about what justice requires. Most are content to capture criminals and allow the justice system to try, convict and imprison them, but others (like the Punisher and the Suicide Squad's Amanda Waller) take a more direct approach, often functioning as judge, jury and executioner. *Fairness* is another important facet of justice. In general, individuals should be treated the same unless there's a morally relevant reason to treat them differently. In Western societies, discrimination based on race, gender, sexual orientation, etc. is now widely recognized as wrong (although it still occurs, sometimes in very subtle and insidious ways). In the Marvel Universe, prejudice against mutants — and, more recently, **Inhumans** — has long been used as an analogy for real-life forms of discrimination.

CONFIRMATION BIAS AND MOTIVATED REASONING. Confirmation Bias and Motivated Reasoning are major contributors to our intellectual vices. All of us fall prey to these cognitive biases; we need to be constantly vigilant to avoid their distorting influence. They derive from our tendency to favor evidence that supports (confirms) our established views and deny or marginalize evidence that contradicts them. Studies have consistently shown that our values and beliefs strongly influence how we interpret information. If, for example, we're convinced that Spider-Man is a menace rather than a hero, we'll construe his actions in the worst possible light. If he saves ten passengers from a bus that's thrown off the Brooklyn Bridge, we'll focus on the fact that he allowed public property to be destroyed and cost taxpayers tens of thousands of dollars. Moreover, we'll actively week out information that supports our beliefs. (Instead of reading news stories that accurately report Spider-Man's activities we'll bookmark J. Jonah Jameson's blog, which demonizes him.) This is especially true if the beliefs in question are strongly held and comprise an important part of our identity.

❷ **Think of an opinion you hold very strongly. If you conducted an Internet search which was related to that belief, would you be equally likely to click on an article that questioned your view as you would on a site that supports it? If you visited the critical site, how open would you be to evidence that directly contradicted your perspective?**

Inhumans (Marvel, 1965). In the distant past, an alien species known as the Kree visited Earth and conducted genetic experiments on early humans. Their descendants, who became known as Inhumans, developed an advanced civilization and lived in isolation from the rest of humanity. When young Inhumans are exposed to a substance known as Terrigen Mist, their full genetic potential is unlocked and they manifest superhuman abilities. The Inhumans are ruled over by their king, Black Bolt, and their queen, Medusa. Other prominent Inhumans include Crystal (Medusa's sister), Gorgon, Karnak, Triton, and Lockjaw (who resembles a large bulldog and can teleport himself and others long distances). ⊗

VARIETIES OF JUSTICE. Philosophers have drawn a distinction between *distributive justice* and *retributive justice*. The principles of distributive justice govern how goods (wealth, power, possessions) are distributed in society. Does everyone deserve the same opportunity to succeed in society regardless of the circumstances of their birth – i.e., whether they're born into a rich family or a poor one, whether they're black or white, male or female, etc. – or should we simply accept differences in life chances as the "luck of the draw"? If society *is* obligated to help compensate for disadvantages, what methods should it use? Does everyone need to *end up* with the same amount of resources, or is the system fair as long as everyone has an equal *chance* to succeed? Retributive justice concerns questions of punishment. Should punishment of wrong-doing be based on *retribution* – individuals who break society's rules deserves to suffer as a consequence of their actions – or should it focus more on *deterrence* (preventing other people from doing wrong) and *rehabilitation* (improving the wrong-doer's moral character so they're less likely to offend again)? In other words, should punishment be oriented in a backward-looking direction – its justification derives from what the wrong-doer has done in the *past* – or a forward-looking one, focused on making the *future* better for both the offender and the broader society? Sometimes these approaches to punishment can overlap with one another. For example, a murderer may *deserve* very harsh punishment (in a retributive sense) and inflicting that punishment may *deter* potential murderers from committing a crime. In other cases, however, they can contradict each other. The vast majority of criminals are eventually released from prison, and if society's demand for retribution deprives them of an opportunity to improve themselves while they're incarcerated (e.g., by withholding access to drug treatment and education), they're likely to reoffend once they're out. φ

❷ Do you think our society provides equal opportunity (the same chance to be successful) for all its citizens, regardless of their race, social class, gender, disability, etc.? If not, what (if anything) should we do to make the "playing field" fairer? In your view, what's the primary purpose of punishment? Does our criminal justice system fulfill this purpose? If not, what changes would you propose?

John Rawls (1921 – 2002). Rawls was an American political philosopher who is best known for his 1971 book, *A Theory of Justice*. It includes a famous thought experiment that he called the Original Position. According to Rawls, when trying to envision a morally just (fair and equitable) society we should imagine that we don't know what position we would occupy in that society: we should view it from behind a "Veil of Ignorance." Such a society would not include the institution of slavery, because we might end up being enslaved ourselves, nor would it systematically discriminate on the basis of race, gender, sexual orientation, etc. since we might (hypothetically) belong to one of these disadvantaged groups. Instead, every individual should have a roughly equal chance to achieve his or her full potential regardless of the circumstances of their birth. In Rawls' view, justice doesn't require complete equality in terms of outcomes – some people will be more successful than others by virtue of good luck, hard work, higher intelligence, etc. However, his Difference Principle states that any policy that results in inequalities is only justified if it helps the worst off. For example, lower tax rates for the wealthy should only be permitted if it can be demonstrated that the rich will invest more money in the economy, creating jobs that benefit citizens with the most disadvantages. *Superpower: Devising ingenious "thought experiments" which can change the way we understand fundamental issues.* ф

Compassion

Compassion is also central to the ethical life. If someone acts on the basis of compassion, she understands the pain or frustration that someone else is experiencing and is moved to help. As social animals, humans are hard-wired to feel sympathy for others (with the exception of psychopaths like the Joker). **Wonder Woman** (aka Diana, an Amazonian warrior princess) demonstrates great compassion. She left Paradise Island, an isolated utopian society, after she became aware of the outside world. Diana dedicated herself to relieving human suffering. She even feels compassion for her enemies, striving to resolve conflicts without the use violence whenever possible. Heroes with empathic abilities (like **Raven**, a member of the **Teen Titans** who is the daughter of a demon; and **Jean Gray**, an X-Man with telepathic powers) can *literally* feel the emotions of others.

Wonder Woman (DC, 1942). Diana was sculpted from clay by her mother Hippolyta on the mythical island of Themyscira, which men are forbidden to visit. Given life by the Greek gods, Diana had an idyllic childhood and was beloved by her mother and fellow Amazons. When the outside world intruded on the isolated paradise of Themyscira with the arrival of military pilot Steve Trevor, Diana decided to leave her home and use her divinely-given abilities to fight evil. She became known as Wonder Woman. A member of the Justice League, Wonder Woman possesses incredible strength, speed, and agility, along with the ability to fly. She wears indestructible bracelets and wields a golden lasso that can force people who are bound by it to tell the truth. ⊗

The Teen Titans (DC, 1964). The Teen Titans are a super-group consisting of young heroes, many of whom served as "sidekicks" of members of the Justice League. Membership has varied over the years but has usually included Robin, Kid Flash, Wonder Girl and Superboy. The character of **Raven** was introduced in 1980. The daughter of a demon named Trigon and a human mother, she was raised in an alternate dimension and taught to suppress her demonic powers. When Trigon threatened to invade the Earth, Raven allied herself with the Teen Titans and helped them defeat her father. Raven possesses the ability to manipulate mystical energy, which she can use to teleport herself and others long distances. She's also a powerful empath: she can sense and control the emotions of others, and can heal people who are in physical or psychic distress by absorbing their pain into herself. ⊗

Jean Gray (Marvel, 1963). An original member of the X-Men, Jean Grey is a mutant with the powers of telepathy (she can "read" and control the minds of others) and telekinesis (which enables her to manipulate physical objects at a distance). In a famous story arc, Jean died and was reborn as the Phoenix, inhabited by an immensely powerful cosmic force that granted her nearly limitless power. When her mind was corrupted by the machinations of a villain known as Mastermind, Jean became the "Dark Phoenix" and destroyed an entire star system. Although she ended her own life in order to protect her fellow X-Men and the universe, Jean has returned to life (and died again) multiple times. ⊗

THE LIMITS OF EMPATHY. The concept of *empathy* is closely aligned with the idea of compassion. (The words derive from the languages of Greek and Latin, respectively, and translated literally mean "feeling with.") Empathy is usually defined as "understanding what someone else is feeling," i.e. experiencing the world from their emotional perspective. Like compassion, it's usually regarded as an unmitigated good, inspiring us to perceive the pain of others and help those in need. However, critics of empathy argue that the feelings it inspires are inherently biased and can therefore mislead us. We're more likely to feel empathy for people who are similar to us because we can identify with them more easily. Difference (in terms of race, national identity, language, etc.) and distance (geographical location) create obstacles to empathy: in other words, it's more difficult to care about people who seem "strange" and are far away. Accordingly, "rational compassion" may be a better guide to moral behavior than empathy. Instead of blindly following our emotions, we should carefully consider our options and choose the course of action that will do the most to relieve suffering in the world. ϕ

❓ Imagine you have $50 to spend on charity. Would rather buy Christmas presents for a local family whose parents were recently laid off from their jobs or give it to an international aid agency which assist people in developing countries who suffer from chronic disease and malnutrition? (The agency has been judged to be extremely effective by independent evaluators: the $50 will not be wasted, it will definitely be used to help those in need.) Why? Which choice would actually do more good?

ANECDOTAL EVIDENCE. The human mind is powerfully influenced by memorable instances and evocative stories. Although this tendency isn't necessarily bad, it can mislead us when an anecdote (example) is either false — it didn't actually happen — or unrepresentative, meaning it's an exception rather than the rule. Anecdotes can feed into harmful stereotypes if we had (or heard about or viewed) a negative experience with someone who belongs to an ethnic minority. In these cases, scientifically-validated statistics provide a much better guide. For example, people who are in the U.S. illegally are significantly less likely to commit violent or property crimes than native-born citizens. However, widely publicized stories about "dangerous illegals" can obscure this fact and distort discussions about immigration policy. Similarly, charities have found that requests for donations are far more effective if they focus on individuals in need instead of relying on abstract statistics. If you want to appeal to people who are concerned about global poverty, your advertisement should feature a single starving child rather than charts and graphs depicting the millions of people suffering from starvation around the world. This tactic is only unethical if it misrepresents the issue being addressed. Evocative stories can either mislead or inspire, depending on how they're used. 🖂

Reciprocity

When combined with *compassion*, the value of *reciprocity* (treating others the way you would like to be treated) provides a firm foundation for ethics. Once we acknowledge that other people are *like us* in their capacity to suffer, experience joy, feel frustrated, and pursue goals, reciprocity enables us to recognize the moral inconsistency of subjecting them to cruel and inhumane treatment. Historically, horrendous crimes such as slavery, the near-extermination of Native Americans, the subjugation of women and the persecution of Jews were "justified" by the belief that their victims were less than fully human: they don't matter morally in the same way that "we" (those in power) do. The mutant Magneto has been depicted as a survivor of the Holocaust, the attempt by the Nazi Party to wipe out European Jews. His tireless campaign to protect mutants against persecution is motivated, in part, by his memories of the concentration camps. Unfortunately, Magneto comes to believe that mutants are not just equal to other humans, they're superior (*homo sapiens* vs. *homo superior*) – which leads him to justify atrocities of his own.

THE GOLDEN RULE. The "Golden Rule" enshrines the moral ideal of *reciprocity* – you should treat others the way you'd like to be treated – and is found in every major world religion. Based on this principle, it's ethically inconsistent and impermissible to subject other people to treatment that you, yourself, would not want to experience. If you don't want to be murdered, you shouldn't commit murder; if you don't want to be enslaved, you shouldn't own slaves; etc. If it's applied too literally, however, the Golden Rule can justify immoral behavior. In a story arc that led to the first Marvel superhero Civil War, the actions of a hero named **Speedball** and his teammates resulted in the death of over six hundred innocent people. Haunted by this tragedy, Speedball abandoned his fun-loving, goofy persona and adopted the guise of a much darker hero known as **Penance**. He wore a suit with 612 inward facing spikes (representing the number of victims) and used that pain to fuel his powers. In his case, then, the Golden Rule could justify the imposition of awful pain on others. To avoid this conclusion, some philosophers have advocated a modified version of reciprocity called the *Platinum Rule*: treat others the way *they* want to be treated, not necessarily the way *you* would want to be treated.

(Of course, this could still be problematic if an individual is mentally ill or otherwise self-destructive.) φ

Speedball/Penance (Marvel, 1988). As a teenager, Robbie Baldwin was exposed to extra-dimensional energy during a scientific experiment gone wrong. Now possessing the ability to generate "kinetic energy fields," he became a superhero known as Speedball. Baldwin eventually joined the New Warriors, a team comprised of other young heroes. In a tragic story arc that led to the first superhero Civil War, a battle between the Warriors and a super-villain known as Nitro resulted in a massive explosion that killed over 600 civilians. Overcome by guilt, Baldwin reemerged as Penance and became a member of the Thunderbolts. He ultimately made peace with his past and resumed his Speedball persona. Speedball can generate force bubbles that protect him from harm and can redirect the force of any attack in another direction. ⊗

MORAL LUCK. Does the morality of an action depend more on the *intentions* of the person acting or on the *consequences* of her action? If intention is all that matters, then Speedball (to cite the example discussed above) has no reason to feel guilty. His intention was identical to that of every other superhero: he wanted to use his powers to help people in need. The effect, however, was as catastrophic as it was unforeseen. Morally speaking, what's the difference between Robbie Baldwin and Peter Parker? Although Spider-Man has made mistakes, they've never resulted in the death of hundreds of innocent people. The difference was a matter of luck (i.e., random chance): Baldwin and his companions did their best to stop Nitro without causing "collateral damage" but events conspired against them. (Many characters in the Marvel Universe have the superhuman ability to change circumstances in their favor — including the Black Cat, Domino, Longshot and the Scarlet Witch — but Speedball is unfortunately not among them.) Consider a more realistic example. If someone is drunk and gets behind the wheel of a car, luck determines whether he gets home safely. If his luck is good he'll arrive home without incident despite his impaired driving; if his luck is bad he'll get into an accident, injuring and perhaps even killing himself and others. In terms of *intention*, the actions of each person are exactly the same. The results only differ because of factors outside the driver's control. Does that mean punishment for drinking and driving should be equally severe regardless of whether someone gets hurt? What if someone is sober but gets distracted while driving because he's checking his cell phone or eating food? Again, *luck* determines whether the consequences of his irresponsibility are trivial or catastrophic. On a deeper level, all of us were all lucky (in a moral sense) that we weren't born in Germany in 1915. If we were adult citizens of Germany when the Nazis came to power we would be faced with the agonizing decision of whether to join, tolerate or resist the Nazi Party. We might like to *think* we'd oppose Hitler and help our Jewish neighbors, but a vanishingly small percentage of Germans did so – the vast majority either remained silent or actively participated in the carnage. Under similar circumstances, chances are that most of us would do the same. Hopefully our luck will last and we'll never have to find out! ϕ

❓ Do you think the punishment for drinking and driving should be the same regardless of whether or not the offender causes an accident? Why or why not?

Courage

Courage is another fundamental value: boldness and a refusal to back down in the face of danger. Courage can be both physical (putting oneself in bodily jeopardy) and moral (standing up for a principle in the face of opposition). Heroes routinely show both kinds of courage. For example, the reality-shaping powers of Green Lanterns (an intergalactic corps of space-cops) are based on their ability to overcome great fear. In the absence of courage, a Lantern's power ring is simply an emerald accouterment. Likewise, **Captain America** is renowned for his courage: he always perseveres, even in the face of seemingly impossible odds. Even before the super-soldier formula transformed his body he possessed the moral virtue of never giving up. However, in some ways courage is a morally "neutral" value since it can be directed toward immoral ends. Although many villains are cowardly, using trickery (like Thor's brother Loki) or terroristic tactics (e.g., threatening innocent people) to defeat their enemies, some exhibit actual courage.

Captain America (Marvel, 1941). Born in 1920 in New York City, Steve Rogers volunteered to serve in the U.S. Army during World War Two but was rejected due to his physical frailty. Recognizing the strength of his character, a scientist named Abraham Erskine selected him for the military's "Super Soldier" program. Rogers was transformed into a perfect physical specimen, but Erskine was assassinated before any other volunteers could undergo the procedure. In order to inspire American troops fighting on the front lines Rogers was given a star-spangled uniform and called Captain America. He fought bravely throughout the war alongside his sidekick Bucky Barnes, but both he and Bucky were presumed dead when a plane they were on exploded in mid-air. It was later revealed that Rogers was frozen, spending the next several decades in suspended animation. (Bucky was saved by the Soviets and brainwashed into becoming as assassin known as the Winter Soldier.) When he was finally resuscitated in the modern world, Captain America became a superhero and a frequent member of the Avengers. Although he represents American values, he often operates independent of the government and will oppose its representatives when he believes they're wrong. Rogers is a highly skilled fighter who wields a virtually unbreakable shield cast from the fictional metals vibranium and adamantium. ⊗

Honesty

Honesty is universally recognized as a core moral value: we should be truthful with other people and avoid intentionally deceiving them. Some of us are scrupulously (or brutally) honest, always telling the truth no matter what the consequences. Others are pathological liars, lying instinctively and at every opportunity. Most of us, of course, fall somewhere in between these extremes: we generally demonstrate the virtue of honesty but sometimes deceive others, usually to avoid negative consequences for ourselves. However, is it also possible that lying can be *virtuous* (morally good)? Consider the question of *secret identities*. Although some superheroes (like the members of the Fantastic Four) openly share their civilian names with the world, the vast majority of them keep their real identities secret. Audiences are obviously aware that Clark Kent is Superman, Peter

Great Responsibility

Parker is Spider-Man, etc., but very few people within their fictional worlds are privy to that information. Heroes often conceal the truth even from those who are closest to them, such as Spider-Man's beloved Aunt May. Why? To protect them. If a hero's enemies find out who they really are, their loved ones are in great danger of being targeted and used against them. For example, Batman's butler Alfred (who raised Bruce Wayne after his parents were murdered and also serves as a father figure, medic, voice of reason, etc.) has often been kidnapped by villains: in one story line he was abducted by the Joker, who proceeded to cut off Alfred's hand! So, heroes with secret identities deceive the world (and, often, their loved ones themselves) in order to protect the people who matter most to them. Is this a *virtuous* form of deception?

EGOISM VS. ALTRUISM. *Egoism* is a term philosophers use for selfishness, i.e. acting in your self-interest without caring how your behavior impacts other people. In most cases, lying is motivated by egoism: we deceive others to get what we want. In some cases, however, we lie to help others – for example, to spare their feelings. Based on our motivation, actions like lying can be placed on a spectrum of self-interest from pure egoism at one extreme (we have zero regard for how others are impacted) to pure altruism at the other. *Altruism* refers to behavior that entails the sacrifice of our own interests on behalf of others. In other words, we completely disregard what we want and are exclusively motivated by the desire to help. Most of our actions fall somewhere between these two extremes, i.e. are driven by a mixture of egoism (what's good for us) and altruism (what's good for others). According to the theory of *Psychological Egoism*, altruism is impossible: everything humans do is motivated by self-interest. Even when people *seem* to be sacrificing their own interests – e.g., by risking their life to save a stranger – they're actually driven by their subconscious desires (such as achieving fame or avoiding guilt). While Psychological Egoism is a psychological theory (an idea about how the human mind works), *Moral Egoism* is an ethical theory. Proponents of Moral Egoism acknowledge that altruism is possible but deny that it's desirable. They claim that individuals *should* behave selfishly: when faced when an ethical decision, you should always act in a way that serves your own interests regardless of how other people are affected. ф

---

❷ Do you think that Psychological Egoism is true? Why or why not? Assuming Altruism is, in fact, possible – in other words, that Psychological Egoism is false – do you regard Moral Egoism as an appealing ethical theory? Is selfishness a moral virtue?

Ayn Rand (1905 – 1982). Born and raised in Russia, the woman who became known as Ayn Rand moved to the U.S. in 1926. Rejecting the collectivism of the Soviet Union – her father's business was confiscated by the state after the Communist Revolution – she developed a philosophy called Objectivism, which she outlined in a series of essays and in popular novels like *The Fountainhead* and *Atlas Shrugged*. Rand was an atheist and argued that ethical behavior should be guided by rational self-interest, a form of Moral Egoism. In her view, our overriding moral obligation is to promote our own well-being: although altruism (self-sacrifice on behalf of others) is *possible*, it's morally destructive. Society will flourish if every individual pursues his or her own good; it will suffer, decline and ultimately collapse if it's weakened by the false values of compassion and selflessness. Rand was a staunch defender of Capitalism and opposed any form of Socialism. Although her work is not highly regarded by most philosophers, it's inspired many politicians (including U.S. Representative Ron Paul, who named his son – currently a Senator from Kentucky – Rand) and libertarian activists. *Superpower: Making selfishness seem like a moral virtue!* φ

Conflicting Values

This list of values is obviously incomplete; many others (including liberty, loyalty, integrity, tolerance and mercy) could be added. Although all of these values are broadly accepted both within societies and among different cultures, they're often understood and applied in different ways. We've already seen how the Punisher's vision of *justice* differs from that of less punitive heroes and how *honesty* isn't as straightforward as one might initially assume. To further complicate the moral situation, values sometimes conflict with each other. As with conflicting obligations, we're forced to decide which value should take precedence in deciding how we ought to proceed. Imagine that Aunt May gives her nephew Peter an extremely ugly sweater for Christmas. *Honesty* would compel him to tell her the truth — unless the *Daily Bugle* has an ugly-sweater office party he'll probably never wear it — but *compassion* might lead him to lie out of concern for her feelings. Which value should trump the other? This is a simple and trivial example, but values can also conflict in more significant ways. In Marvel's Civil War cross-over series (which served as a loose inspiration for the Captain America movie of the same name), heroes were split over the Superhuman Registration Act (equivalent to the Sokovia Accords in the cinematic universe). After a super-powered battle in a small town in Connecticut caused the death of hundreds of innocent people, the federal government passed a law requiring all heroes to register their real names and subject themselves to training and supervision. One group of heroes (led by **Iron Man**) supported the law and the *legal obligation* it created, acting out of compassion for the victims of the tragedy and a powerful sense of justice. The opposing group (led by Captain America) believed that the law violated the liberty of heroes and placed too much power in the hands of the government; they interpreted *justice* (what people deserve) in a very different way. Ultimately they resolved their conflict by fighting each other, as heroes often do; violence may be unavoidable if two sides are unable to peacefully resolve fundamental moral differences.

IN-GROUP BIAS. The human mind has an innate (built-in, hard-wired) tendency to like and trust people who seem similar to us, and we're prone to dislike and distrust anyone we deem to be different. This "us vs. them" mindset is extraordinarily powerful and can be activated by trivial differences (e.g., which group we were randomly assigned to by a person conducting an experiment). When attached to deeper aspects of our identity — nationality, ethnicity, religion, race, gender, sexual orientation, political affiliation, etc. — it can distort our thinking in profound ways and, at the extreme, serve as a pretext for discrimination or even atrocities. In political debates, studies have shown that many Americans are more concerned with conforming to their group (e.g., Republicans or Democrats) than maintaining a consistent and principled moral perspective. We're likely to oppose a position we supported in the past if our party turns against it and the other party ends up adopting it. 🖦

❓ **Can you think of any ways in which you've been influenced by in-group bias? If not, can you point out examples among others, either people you know personally or have seen in the media?**

Iron Man (Marvel, 1963). Tony Stark was a wealthy businessman who was kidnapped by a group of terrorists. Although his captors tried to force him to construct a weapon, Stark built a suit of armor instead and used it to escape. After improving and upgrading the armor he emerged as Iron Man, a founding member of the Avengers. In addition to being a superhero, Stark is the CEO of Stark Enterprises, a highly successful company that specializes in advanced technologies. Iron Man's armor protects him from harm, enables him to fly, and includes a variety of weapon systems. Over the years Stark has developed countless different versions of the armor, some of which are highly specialized and can be operated by remote control. He's also given versions of the armor to his colleagues James Rhodes (who became the hero known as War Machine) and Pepper Potts (who served as Rescue). ⊗

"Everyone is necessarily the hero of his own life story."
— Novelist John Barth

When heroes fight one another, the conflict almost always derives from different conceptions of what justice requires. Daredevil and the Punisher are equally convinced that their approach to fighting crime is the correct one and that his counterpart is foolish, deluded and counter-productive. The same was true of Captain America and Iron Man during the Civil War story arc — and of the leaders of the North and South in the *actual* Civil War. Many villains undoubtedly see themselves as "heroes" as well. Magneto thinks the X-Men are hopelessly naive: peaceful coexistence is impossible, and only *power* will prevent the mutants from becoming victims of persecution. (In the real world, there's a parallel debate in the state of Israel about the best approach to making peace with the Palestinians and safeguarding Israelis from their enemies in the Arab world.) Of course, some villains (like the bank-robbing Rhino) are merely selfish; they just want to get rich. They may think the world has mistreated them and they therefore "deserve" what they're taking, but they can't plausibly regard themselves as heroic. Others — like the Joker — are pure psychopaths. They might *believe* they're serving a higher purpose (for example, in some depictions the Joker thinks he's helping Batman achieve his full potential), but they're obviously deranged.

Likewise, Osama bin Laden believed he was doing God's work by founding the terrorist organization al Qaeda and carrying out horrific attacks on civilian targets. He thought his actions were justified by the intervention of the U.S. and other Western powers in Muslim countries: we often supported brutal dictatorships to protect our "interests" (including access to oil) in the region. Bin Laden was undeniably evil, but he didn't *see himself* that way. Without justifying his actions in any way, it's worth trying to understand his perspective so we can prevent other extremists from following the same path. If it's possible to have some degree of empathy for moral monsters like bin Laden, surely we can extend the same consideration to political opponents in our own society. In recent years there's been an increasing tendency for Democrats and Republicans to demonize the other side. Instead of regarding each other as well-meaning fellow citizens with different ideas of what's best for the country, we condemn the opposition as enemies who are out to destroy America. (The polarizing effect of social media is partly to blame for this trend.) This makes collaboration and compromise impossible to achieve. We would do well to remember that we share most of the same values with our fellow Americans — we simply interpret and seek to apply them differently. Our opponents should not be seen as enemies, but as competitors who share the same goal of helping our country achieve its full potential. Debate should be vigorous but respectful, hard-fought but ultimately productive.

Jonathan Haidt (1963 — present). A social psychologist who specializes in ethical thinking, Haidt (with the help of his colleagues) has developed a theory of moral foundations. According to this view, moral systems are based on six basic principles: *care* (practicing kindness, compassion and empathy; the opposite is *harm*); *fairness* (upholding justice, rights and equality; *cheating*); *loyalty* (demonstrating commitment to one's group; *betrayal*); *authority* (following established rules and respecting tradition; *subversion*); *sanctity* (striving to maintain purity and nobility in how we live; *degradation*); and *liberty* (allowing individuals to make their own decisions; *oppression*). Psychological research has found that political conservatives tend to support all six principles, with particular focus on loyalty, authority and sanctity. Liberals, in contrast, rely almost exclusively on care, fairness and liberty in forming their moral views. This can result in fundamental disagreement on a wide range of ethical issues, e.g. the moral status of homosexuality. Most liberals believe that society should tolerate or even celebrate gays and lesbians: they're not hurting anyone (no *harm* is being done) and should therefore have the *liberty* to live as they choose. It's *unfair* and *uncaring* to discriminate against them. Although some conservatives accept this argument, others aren't convinced — especially conservative Christians. From their perspective, we're obligated to accept the *authority* of the Bible (which, in their view, clearly condemns homosexuality) and must defend the *sanctity* of both sex (they regard gay sex as unnatural and disgusting) and marriage. Interestingly, the best way to persuade Christians to change their views about homosexuality is through encounters with fellow conservatives who share their values but arrive at a different conclusion. This reflects the importance of *loyalty*: people are more likely to rethink their position if they can do so without abandoning their identity and betraying their group. *Superpower: The capacity to change his mind (Although Haidt was a committed liberal when he began his career, he moderated some of his views after conducting research on conservative perspectives).* φ

❓ What moral values are most important to you, and how exactly do you interpret them? Think of an issue that brings your values into conflict. (For example, respecting the *liberty* of individuals to speak freely vs. *compassion* for people who might feel threatened by what offensive speakers say.) How would you resolve this conflict? In other words, how do you decide which value takes precedence over the others?

WHAT ARE ETHICS? Part Three: Rights and Moral Theories

Values and *obligations* are closely interconnected. For example, obligations can flow from values: we're obligated to treat everyone equally (whether they're white or black, mutant or non-mutant) insofar as we accept the principle of justice. In many cases, laws (like the Superhuman Registration Act) are intended to enforce broadly shared values. In general, however, laws are intended to *prevent us from doing wrong* rather than *force us to do what's right*. You're legally obligated to refrain from taking what doesn't belong to you, but you're not required (by law, at least) to give money to a charity that helps the bystander victims of superhuman battles. Compassion may inspire you to give to this kind of fund (or its real-life equivalent) – by generating a *humanitarian obligation* – but you won't be punished if you refuse. Interestingly, superheroes who are vigilantes (i.e., they're not officially sanctioned by the government) routinely violate their *legal obligations* to serve what they regard as a higher good. Do we have the right (or even the requirement) to break the law if we think it's unjust, or if it gets in the way of achieving what we regard as a more important moral goal? If everyone thought this way, society might collapse into chaos. On the other hand, moral progress has often been made by movements (abolitionists opposed to slavery, suffragettes who fought for women's right to vote, civil rights activists who opposed segregation and discrimination, etc.) that challenge and ultimately transform the status quo. Likewise, Europeans who hid Jews from the Nazis were violating the law but are regarded – in retrospect – as moral heroes.

Rights

Rights are another important and related moral concept. If I have the *right* to do something, then others (the government, fellow citizens, etc.) are obligated to refrain from interfering with me. First and foremost, rights establish limits on the power of the state over its citizens. In some cases, however, governments need to protect individuals from having their rights infringed by *other* citizens or by corporations. For example, the right to free speech means I can express myself however I choose; freedom of religion enables me to believe and worship as I see fit. However, rights are never absolute: they're always limited and context-dependent. Although the First Amendment guarantees my liberty to say what I want, certain statements (e.g., threats on the life of the President or speech which openly advocates violence) are not permitted. In comic-book terms, I can say that mutants are "gene-jokes" who pose a grave danger to "normal" humans, but I can't (legally) promote the idea that we should create mutant-hunting robots to wipe them off the face of the earth. Likewise, my religious liberty ends when my actions threaten to directly harm other people. Batman's archrival **Ra's al Ghul** is free to *believe* that humans are enemies of the planet and must be driven extinct to preserve what remains of the natural world, but he's not allowed to release a plague that kills hundreds in Gotham City and threatens to wipe out humanity. Another example: when criminal suspects are arrested they have "the right to remain silent" to avoid incriminating themselves by admitting their crime. Unlike police officers, who are usually careful to fulfill their *professional obligations*, superheroes almost never read criminals their Miranda rights — nor do they obtain a warrant before searching for evidence of a crime. Unless the principles of due process are very different in the Marvel and DC Universes, prosecutors must have a very difficult time convicting criminals who are captured by superheroes!

Ra's al Ghul (DC, 1971). Born centuries ago into a tribe of nomads in the Arabian desert, the man who became known as Ra's al Ghul (which means "the head of the demon" in Arabic) discovered a "Lazurus Pit," which grants humans immortality. Over his long life, Ra's came to believe that humans are a cancer on the planet who are destroying its natural balance and beauty. He founded a vast, shadowy organization known as the Demon and leads a group of killers known as the League of Assassins. His attempts to massively reduce the human population have been repeatedly foiled by Batman. Ra's is the grandfather of Bruce Wayne's son, Damian, who is currently serving in the role of Robin. He is a genius who has mastered numerous scientific disciplines and fighting methods. Regular exposure to the Lazarus Pits has endowed him with enhanced physical attributes. ⊗

The rights I've discussed so far involve the right to be left alone: i.e., other people are obligated to allow me to think, say and do what I want (within carefully defined limits). We also refer to *rights* that entitle us to certain goods or privileges. For example, many people believe that society (usually acting through the government) has the *civic obligation* to guarantee a basic level of education, sustenance, shelter and health care to all its citizens. As mentioned earlier, libertarians reject this claim: at the extreme, they argue that all taxation is a form of theft and insist that charitable contributions should only be made voluntarily. More broadly, they want to maximize individual freedom and minimize the size and scope of the government. In their view, the government exceeds its proper boundaries when it takes over services (like education and health care) that are better provided by the private sector.

Libertarians are right to be concerned about the danger of excessive government power, as demonstrated by a Marvel story line set on an alternate-reality Earth. There, the **Squadron Supreme** – a super-group very similar to DC's Justice League, with counterparts to Superman, Wonder Woman, Batman, etc. – use their powers to take over the United States government. Instead of focusing on the *symptoms* of social problems (by fighting crime), they address the *root causes* of human suffering in order create a kind of utopia, where hunger, violence, scarcity and criminality have been virtually eliminated. However, their use of a behavior modification device (which changes the brains of criminals so they're incapable of committing future crimes) causes several of the Squadron's members to turn against them, leading a rebellion on behalf of individual freedom. Ultimately, **Hyperion** (an analogue to DC's Superman) realizes his mistake and relinquishes power. Do you agree with his decision, or would you trade your individual rights for a world without unnecessary suffering?

HUMAN RIGHTS. Since the middle of the 20th century, the international community has recognized (in theory, if not always in practice) that every human being possesses certain fundamental rights regardless of how their society may treat them. The Universal Declaration of Human Rights was drafted after the horrors of World War II were fully revealed, in part to justify the prosecution of Nazis who committed atrocities and claimed that they were simply following orders. Echoing the U.S. Declaration of Independence, the Charter proclaims that "all human beings are born free and equal in dignity and rights." It proceeds to summarize the specific rights all people possess: freedom of life, liberty, security, movement, thought, belief, expression, political participation, and due process under law. These are examples of *liberty rights* (also called "negative rights"), the right to make one's own decisions without undue interference from the government or other citizens. More controversially, the Charter also affirms a set of *welfare rights* (aka "positive rights"), including the right to work, leisure, health care, social support, education, and participation in cultural activities. According to some critics, individuals are not entitled to receive these benefits from society: they need to be earned or provided by voluntary charities. φ

❷ Do you think that people possess welfare rights? If so, is the *government* obligated to make sure that people receive what they need, or should provision of food, health care, etc. for the disadvantaged be left up to charity?

SLIPPERY SLOPE. A *slippery slope* argument takes the following form: If we allow *this* to happen (i.e., if we make a small concession to our political opponents), then a catastrophic consequence will inevitably occur. This kind of argumentation is fallacious if there's a logical stopping point between the initial step and the ultimate result. For example, opponents of laws which restrict gun ownership sometimes argue that *any* infringement on their right to possess arms will likely lead to the confiscation of *all* guns and, perhaps, the transformation of America into a totalitarian state. They point to examples like Nazi Germany (which prohibited Jews from owning guns, not all citizens) and the U.S.S.R. under Stalin, in which gun control preceded the persecution and mass killing of civilians. Although it's true that oppressive regimes will attempt to disarm the parts of the population that they're targeting, it doesn't follow that gun control laws will necessarily lead to the same result. In the U.S., for example, the right to own firearms is enshrined in the Second Amendment to the Constitution and supported by virtually all politicians. Despite scare mongering on the part of gun advocacy groups like the NRA, gun ownership is not endangered by modest reforms like universal background checks for gun buyers and restrictions on certain kinds of assault weapons. Of course, these measures might not meaningfully reduce the number gun deaths either — that's an open question. However, the debate should not be distorted by false and frightening claims. ☁

❓ Slippery slope arguments were also used against the legalization of gay marriage. What arguments did opponents of marriage equality make, and how did supporters respond? Has subsequent history proven that one of the sides was correct?

The Squadron Supreme (Marvel, 1971). A thinly-veiled homage to the Justice League, the Squardon Supreme inhabits an alternate-reality version of the Marvel Universe and includes counterparts to all of the DC team's characters: Superman (Hyperion), Batman (Nighthawk), Wonder Woman (Power Princess), Aquaman (Amphibian), Green Lantern (Doctor Spectrum) and the Flash (Whizzer). A villainous version of the group, known as the Squadron Sinister, occupies yet another alternate world. Both teams were created as a foil to the Avengers, whom they encountered when they crossed over into the "real" Marvel Universe. However, the Squadron's own world was explored on its own terms in an acclaimed 1985 mini-series. Supported by most of his teammates, Hyperion instituted a "Utopia Program" which effectively abolished poverty, criminality and violence. He was opposed by Nighthawk and several other former members of the team, who argued that the "utopia" the Squadron has created was not worth the loss of individual freedom and the danger of future dictators abusing their power. Nighthawk was killed in battle, leading Hyperion to realize his mistake and dismantle the Program. ⊗

Moral Theories

(Unavoidably, this entire section features specialized philosophical terms and will be confined to "digging deeper" text boxes.)

UTILITARIANISM AND DEONTOLOGY. *Utilitarianism* (from the root word *utility*, or "usefulness") is a form a *consequentialism*, which means that the rightness or wrongness of an action depends on its likely consequences. In contrast, *Deontology* (from the Greek *deon*, which means "duty" – it's also known as *Duty Ethics*) is a rule-based system which claims that actions are right and wrong in themselves, regardless of the consequences. When Utilitarians are faced with a moral question, they choose the option that is likely to result in the "greatest good" (often defined as maximizing pleasure and minimizing pain) for everyone who is affected by the decision. Deontologists, in contrast, will apply the moral rules that they uphold, even if the results are mixed or even harmful. For example, most Utilitarians will decide whether to lie based on the specific circumstances. If someone is lying for a purely selfish reason (to avoid getting in trouble, for example), that's clearly wrong. If, however, a lie is likely to benefit everyone who's affected by it – including the person being lied to – than it may be morally justified. The "pros" and "cons" need to be weighed up for each situation, and the morally correct choice is whichever option seems likely to lead to the better outcome. Conversely, if a Deontologist believes that lying is morally wrong – i.e., we have an ethical duty to tell the truth under all circumstances – then she is obligated to be honest regardless of the likely outcome. When Deontologists confront choices that involve conflicting duties, they're forced to decide which duty takes precedence (e.g., the duty to tell the truth may conflict with the duty to protect innocent life.) In many cases, Utilitarians and Deontologists will reach the same ethical conclusion, but the reasons underlying their decision will be different. In other cases the application of these moral theories leads to very different outcomes, e.g. whether it's ever morally justified to torture someone in order to save innocent lives. ϕ

❓ Overall, which moral theory – Utilitarianism or Deontology – do you find more appealing? Do you think that there are moral absolutes (actions which are *always* wrong regardless of the consequences), or does ethical reasoning always depend on specific circumstances? If there *are* absolutes, what are they?

Immanuel Kant (1724 – 1804). A German philosopher and key thinker of the Enlightenment, Kant (pronounced "Kah-nt," not like "can't") is among the most influential figures in modern philosophy. He made major contributions to the fields of metaphysics (speculation about the nature of the universe), epistemology (the study of knowledge), aesthetics (theories of art), and political philosophy. In the area of ethics, he's best known as an advocate of a strict Deontological system. Kant argued that our moral duty can be determined through reason alone and that ethics is necessarily universal: the same principles apply to all people in all times and places. In his view, we can determine what ethical rules we're obligated to follow by applying two related tests. The first involves universalizability. You should ask whether the rule would result in a contradiction if everyone were to follow it. For example, consider a rule like, "It's permissible to lie whenever I want to avoid bad consequences." If everyone in society lived according to this principle, it would be impossible to trust other people because the very idea of "truth" would be undermined. The second criterion involves treating people as ends in themselves, not merely as a means to our end. In other words, it's impermissible to use people in ways that fail to acknowledge the fact that they, like you, are rational individuals who are worthy of respect. A rule that allows you to lie whenever it's convenient for you also fails this test, because deception is intended to manipulate people by actively misleading them or withholding relevant information. Accordingly, Kant concluded that lying is never permissible: we have an absolute duty to tell the truth under all circumstances. From Kant's perspective, the *intention* behind an action (i.e., whether we have accurately understood our obligation and are fulfilling it for duty's sake) is more important than its consequences. We should force ourselves to do the right thing even if the results could be harmful to ourselves or others. Finally, Kant believed that emotions are irrelevant to ethics: we should determine our duty by logic alone. In fact, if we feel good after helping someone else, that actually *undermines* the morality of providing assistance because our motivation is no longer pure. *Superpower: Extraordinary punctuality! (Kant supposedly took a walk at the exact same time every day in his hometown of Konisberg; townsfolk said you could set you clock by the time he passed by.)* ϕ

John Stuart Mill (1806 – 1873). Mill was a Utilitarian philosopher and member of Parliament who advocated for many social reforms, including women's suffrage and worker's rights. He wrote a highly influential book entitled *On Liberty*, which argued that the government is only justified in limiting the liberty of its citizens if their actions are likely to harm other people. He strongly opposed censorship; in his view, freedom of speech is a fundamental right. In contrast to Kant, Mill advocated a consequentialist approach to moral philosophy: the rightness or wrongness of an action is decided by its likely consequences. Mill was a Utilitarian, arguing that ethics should produce "the greatest good for the greatest number." In other words, we should make decisions that are likely to maximize the happiness for everyone impacted by our actions. He rejected both Moral Egoism (the idea that we should only care about our *own* happiness) and Deontology (the view that we should follow a strict set of rules). Instead, Mill claimed that ethical reasoning is both contextual (it depends on specific circumstances) and inexact (we can't always *know* what the results of our choices but are forced to make our "best guess" based on past experiences). In all cases, our overriding obligation is to consider the range of options and choose the one that will result in the most collective well-being. *Superpower: Actually putting philosophical principles into practice!* φ

CRITICISMS OF DUTY ETHICS. (1) Deontology is unrealistic and uncharitable about the motivations behind moral acts. Feelings provide the foundation for many moral beliefs, and (as Virtue Ethicists argue) good people get appropriate pleasure from acting ethically. (2) Deontologists demand that moral principles be universalizable. Only if a principle can apply to all people under all circumstances does it qualify as moral; exceptions are not permitted. According to critics, this standard is excessively strict. For example: although lying is generally wrong, in some cases deception might be more ethical than telling the truth (e.g., if a Nazi is knocking on your door demanding to know whether you're hiding Jews in the attic). (3) The inflexibility of deontology derives, in part, from its indifference to consequences. Although motivation is important in determining morality—e.g., we punish intentional murder much more harshly than accidental homicide—results must also be taken into account.

CRITICISMS OF UTILITARIANISM. (1) Some accuse Utilitarianism of being unrealistic. Can people be expected to perform a complicated utilitarian calculation (compared the overall positive and negative effects of their various options) every time they're faced with a moral decision? Can they even *know* what the effects will be, given the ambiguity and uncertainty of human life? Utilitarians have responded by drawing a distinction between two types of Utilitiarianism, ACT (which evaluates every situation independently) and RULE (which formulates general rules of behavior that, overall, will lead to the greater good). The latter version is less vulnerable to this criticism, and—because it allows exceptions—is more flexible than deontology (see criticism #2, above). (2) Utilitarianism also seems unrealistic in requiring that people be impartial in making ethical decisions, regarding the interests of *everyone* as equally important. For example, it seems unavoidable (and, in many ways, socially beneficial) that parents have greater concern for their own children than they do for someone else's kids. As above, however, act utilitarianism is more vulnerable to this criticism than rule. (3) According to critics, Utilitarianism provides no protection for basic rights and principles of justice. If, for example, one hundred people can be made much better off by severely harming ten people (e.g., by killing them and harvesting their organs for transplant), Act Utilitarians would probably support the policy. Again, however, Rule Utilitarians provide a plausible response: a policy of exploiting people against their will would cause great anxiety, the evil of which would almost certainly outweigh the good of transplanting organs.

MORAL PLURALISM. Many philosophers argue that we should choose and consistently follow only *one* ethical theory (e.g., *either* Utilitarianism *or* Deontology). On the surface this makes sense: these approaches to ethics differ dramatically and often lead to contradictory conclusions. According to Moral Pluralists, however, this view is too simplistic and fails to acknowledge the complexity of actual ethical decisions. On the theoretical level it's easy to be consistent, always following your preferred set of principles no matter where they lead you. In reality, however, life can be messy, ambiguous and conflicted – we're often forced to make concessions and compromises. Moral theories can provide us with varying sets of lenses that enable us to view problems from different perspectives. Utilitarianism may illuminate one aspect of an issue while obscuring another aspect, which Deontology (or Virtue Ethics) can help us understand better. Instead of regarding moral theories as competing ideologies that exclude one another, we can see them as tools in a toolbox that are useful depending on the problem we're facing. ϕ

❷ Think of a moral problem (e.g., whether it's wrong to torture a terrorist to get information about a forthcoming attack) about which Utilitarians and Deontologists would disagree. Describe how their analyses differ and why they arrive at different conclusions. Overall, which view do you find more persuasive?

Superheroes and Ethical Thinking

THE ETHICS OF SUPERHEROES. Very few superheroes have an explicit moral philosophy or engage in ethical reasoning. (At least, not as they're portrayed in the comics and movies. It's possible that some heroes work as moral philosophers in their secret identities!) However, we can draw inferences about their moral views based on their behavior. Obviously, the vast majority of heroes are virtuous: they regularly demonstrate the virtues of courage, compassion, integrity and loyalty. However, most heroes have vices as well: few, if any, are morally perfect – and they would be much less interesting if they were! They sometimes struggle with selfishness, dishonesty, arrogance, etc. – just think of Tony Stark, aka Iron Man. In the end, however, their virtues triumph over their vices; that's what makes them heroes. Heroes are clearly consequentialists, at least to some degree: they care about the *results* of their actions. They would undoubtedly hang up their tights if they weren't actually helping people, or if their attempts to help consistently caused more harm than good. However, most heroes are also Deontologists: there are rules that govern their behavior by establishing lines they're not willing to cross. Most heroes follow a strict code against killing, despite the fact that their enemies inevitably escape from prison and are free to cause more death and destruction. Like most of us, then, superheroes are Moral Pluralists: they derive their ethical principles from a variety of different sources and are forced to decide which values take priority when they conflict. ⊗ φ

WHAT ARE ETHICS? Part Four: Moral Dilemmas

A *moral dilemma* is an ethical challenge with no easy answer. When our obligations or values conflict with one another, when defending one person's rights would violate someone else's rights, when doing "the right thing" could result in a disastrous outcome, we face a *dilemma*. There's no perfect solution to these problems: every option is morally compromised. We're forced to decide which values, obligations, rights, etc. take precedence over the others and choose the least bad alternative. In the most compelling comic-book stories, super-heroes (and sometimes villains!) face dilemmas that they're required to resolve.

FALSE DILEMMA. If you face a *genuine* moral dilemma, you have no good option; you're forced to choose the lesser of two (or more) evils. If you're presented with a *false* dilemma, however, better options are, in fact, available — but they're concealed by a fallacious form of argumentation. For example, imagine that a supporter of the death penalty insisted that we can *either* execute convicted killers *or* let them go. Obviously, there are other possible punishments between those two extremes: life without parole, for example. Legitimate moral disagreements are rarely black and white. If someone claims that there are only two options and one of them is clearly correct, you should look for shades of gray. Real-world problems tend to be complicated and ambiguous, not resolvable by simplistic solutions. 🗨

To kill or not to kill? That is the question

Virtually all super-heroes follow a moral code that forbids killing. Those few who do kill — like the Punisher, Wolverine and Deadpool (Marvel) or Wonder Woman, Green Arrow and the Suicide Squad (DC) — stand out as exceptions. Of course, non-killing heroes are not pacifists; they accept that violence is often necessary to fight crime and save the world. (Given how powerful many heroes are, they must be *extraordinarily* careful to use just enough force to incapacitate their enemies without causing permanent harm.) However, they're unwilling to serve as judge, jury and executioner. Should they be? Consider a character like Batman. Many of his villains are deeply disturbed, including mass murdering madmen like the Joker, Black Mask, Scarecrow and Victor Zsasz. Between them, they've claimed hundreds if not thousands of victims. After Batman foils their schemes and defeats these rogues, they're presumably found "not guilty by reason of insanity" and are remanded to Arkham Asylum for "treatment." They inevitably escape, carrying out schemes that cause many more innocent people to die. Is Batman partially culpable for these deaths? If he's concerned about being criminally prosecuted or suffering damage to his reputation, he could easily make the execution of his enemies look accidental, or only kill them in self-defense. Wouldn't the greater good of Gotham be served if Batman ended the threat of the Joker once and for all rather than sending him yet again through the revolving door of Arkham? Should Batman's strict moral code take precedence over the well-being of the citizens he claims to protect? (Of course, comics creators have more pragmatic reasons for keeping these charismatic villains around: they're compelling and very popular!)

THE INSANITY DEFENSE. "Insanity" is a legal concept, not a psychiatric diagnosis. In most jurisdictions, an offender is considered "insane" if he lacked the capacity to distinguish between right and wrong at the time he committed his crime. This is usually the result of a severe mental impairment or an illness like schizophrenia or bipolar disorder. (The vast majority of people with mental illness do not pose a threat to others; they're far more likely to be the victim of violence themselves than to hurt someone else.) If someone is judged to be "insane," they're not morally or legally culpable for their crime. However, they are not therefore released back into the public! Most offenders who are found "not guilty" due to their mental state spend more time in a psychiatric institution receiving treatment than they would have served in prison had they been convicted. The insanity defense is attempted in less than one percent of criminal cases, and even then it only works about 25% of the time. Defendants who lack a prior diagnosis of mental illness are almost never successful in pleading insanity. In other words, it's extremely difficult to fool the court by "pretending" to be insane in order to avoid incarceration. Psychopaths who commit violent crimes (e.g., notorious serial killers like Ted Bundy and Jeffrey Dahmer) are almost never judged insane. They're fully aware of the difference between right and wrong, but because they lack a conscience they simply don't care about the suffering their victims experience. ϕ

---

❷ Do you think it's possible for someone who does not suffer from a mental illness to become "temporarily" insane? In other words, can an otherwise "sane" person be so overcome with anger, emotion, etc. that they're incapable of thinking clearly?

Eating Planets

Galactus is one of the oldest and most powerful characters in the Marvel Universe. He was introduced in the pages of *The Fantastic Four* when he arrived on Earth to consume it. More a force of nature than an actual villain, Galactus is compelled by his insatiable hunger to destroy whole planets and absorb their energy. Before appearing on Earth, Galactus journeyed to the planet of Zenn-La and prepared to consume that world and its inhabitants. To save Zenn-La (and his beloved Shalla-Bal), a man named Norrin Radd volunteered to become the herald of Galactus if the World-Eater would spare his home. Galactus agreed, imbuing Radd with a portion of his cosmic power and transforming him into the **Silver Surfer**. As herald, the Surfer is tasked with finding planets his master can consume. He served in that role until first encountering the Fantastic Four. Inspired by their heroism and unwilling to let the Earth be destroyed, he rebelled against Galactus and was confined to our planet (instead of being free to roam throughout space) as a punishment. The Surfer is often depicted as a noble character, but were his actions morally defensible? Although he sacrificed himself to save his Zenn-La and later opposed his master in defense of the Earth, in the interim he led Galactus to destroy dozens of other planets. Some of them were uninhabited – the Surfer's preference – but others were not, and their populations were either forced to flee or were annihilated. Is it justifiable to endanger many lives to protect one person (Shalla-Bal) you deeply love? In a recent story arc, a team known as the Ultimates finally resolved the Galactus dilemma by transforming him from the World-Eater into the "Life-Bringer": instead of consuming living planets he now seeds dead ones with life. Should the Surfer have sought a solution like that instead of willingly serving as Galactus' accomplice?

Galactus and the Silver Surfer (Marvel, 1966). Galactus began life as an explorer named Galan in the universe that preceded the present Marvel Universe. He survived the end of the old universe and emerged in the new one as a cosmic being who is compelled to consume whole planets in order to satiate his great hunger. Galactus has employed numerous heralds over his long life, individuals imbued with a small part of his cosmic power who seek out worlds for him to destroy and announce his coming. The Silver Surfer served as one of Galactus' heralds before betraying him. Galactus is extraordinarily powerful; he can use his cosmic power to accomplish almost anything he imagines. Possessing a portion of this power, the Surfer has superhuman strength, endurance and senses. He can travel through space far faster than the speed of light and can manipulate cosmic energy to achieve a variety of effects (including energy beams, defensive shields, healing, and matter transformation). ⊗

FAVORITISM VS. IMPARTIALITY. According to ethical theories like Utilitarianism, we're obligated to be completely impartial (unbiased) in our ethical reasoning. When faced with a moral decision, we should choose whichever option leads to the greatest good for everyone who is affected by our choice. Our well-being and the well-being of our loved ones (friends, family members, etc.) shouldn't count any more in our ethical deliberation than the well-being of strangers who will also be impacted. In other words, individuals we care about have no special claim to our attention. *Humanitarian obligations* (to assist people we don't know) are just as binding as *personal* and *even familial obligations.* Can this be right? Obviously, it's deeply counter-intuitive: we naturally care more about our loved ones than about people we've never met! Most non-Utilitarian philosophers defend this kind of favoritism, for both practical and theoretical reasons. Close relationships *do* matter more in an ethical sense; societies couldn't function if parents didn't show special regard for their children and if friends didn't preferentially help their friends. However, how far should this favoritism extend? The Silver Surfer was willing to participate in the destruction of numerous other civilizations to save his own planet. On a much smaller scale, parents who spend many thousands of dollars to provide their children with the best of everything (including many luxuries that they don't truly need) could have done enormous good if they dedicated that money to helping impoverished children in developing countries. φ

❓ Imagine a scenario in which you're on a sinking ship and can either help your dog or a drowning stranger — which would you save? If the choice were between your child and a stranger the answer would be obvious, but what if you had to choose between your child and ten strangers? Fifty? One hundred? Consider whether your decision is *ethically* justifiable or if you're being guided by emotion.

Sacrificing Millions to Save Billions

Set in an alternate reality of the DC Universe, the *Watchmen* mini-series (later adapted into a movie) features a character known as **Ozymandias**. Convinced that the major global powers were going to destroy themselves (and the rest of the world) in a nuclear war, he devised and implemented a plan to cause a massive explosion in a major American city and blame it on alien invaders. Although millions of people would die in the initial attack, Ozymandias believed that *billions* would be saved: only an external threat could inspire humanity to overcome its ideological differences and unite in opposition to a common foe. Two other characters, **Nite Owl** and **Rorscach**, found out about the plan after it was too late to prevent the explosion. Nite Owl reluctantly agreed to keep Ozymandias' secret, but Rorscach promised to reveal his plot to the world. Could Ozymandias' actions be justified? What if he were correct about the inevitability of nuclear war in the absence of an event like the one he engineered? If you were Nite Owl or Rorscach, what would you do? Do people deserve to know the truth about the attack, or would it be better to maintain secrecy after the damage was already done?

The Watchmen (DC, 1986). *The Watchmen* was set in an alternate history in which Richard Nixon was still President in the mid-1980s and the U.S. was on the brink of nuclear war with the Soviet Union. Vigilantism was outlawed, so most superheroes had either retired (like Nite Owl), gone underground (like Rorschach) or affiliated themselves with the government (like the nearly omnipotent Dr. Manhattan). Ozymandias was a prodigy named Adrian Veidt who became a wealthy celebrity after revealing his true identity to the public. He murdered the vigilante known as the Comedian after the latter uncovered Veidt's plan to fake an alien attack. Although the world depicted in *The Watchmen* was originally separate from the mainstream DC Universe, a recent story arc has brought several characters from the series into contact with Batman, Superman and other popular heroes. ⊗

Is Vigilantism Morally Justified?

Does the very decision to become a superhero present a moral dilemma? As we've seen, the vast majority of costumed superheroes are vigilantes: they operate without legal sanction, routinely breaking the law themselves in pursuit of what they regard as "justice." Although some heroes are employed by the government, they're few and far between. Spider-Man is regularly portrayed as a "menace" in the pages of the *Daily Bugle* newspaper due to J. Jonah Jameson's distrust of so-called "heroes." Is he right? Although it's obviously true that Spider-Man and other superheroes do far more good than harm, is their approach inherently immoral? In the real world, the answer would probably be yes. Vigilantism is routinely condemned. However good their intentions, average citizens lack the training that police officers receive and are therefore even *more* likely to commit the kind of errors (often based on racial prejudice) that police officers sometimes make.

As an instructive example, consider the tragic events that unfolded in 2012 when a neighborhood watch coordinator named George Zimmerman confronted a young black man, Trayvon Martin, who was returning home from a convenience store. Zimmerman had a history of calling the police to report "suspicious" persons – all of whom were black. Although the 911 operator told Zimmerman to stop following Martin and wait for the police to arrive, Zimmerman (who was armed with a gun) exited his car and confronted Martin. An ensuing struggle resulted in Martin's death. Although very few people regard Zimmerman as a "hero," the jury in his trial for killing Martin decided that he acted in self-defense. Would society be safer with more people like Zimmerman patrolling the streets? It seems unlikely. Although it's sometimes impractical to wait for the police to arrive if you or your family are in a dangerous situation, self-appointed vigilantes should not arm themselves with deadly weapons and go looking for trouble.

On the other hand, consider the actions of three men who stopped a potentially deadly terrorist attack on a passenger train in 2015. (Their story is the subject of the film *15:17 to Paris*, in which they played themselves.) A terrorist armed with an assault weapon opened fire on the train, intending to inflict mass casualties. The men tackled and incapacitated the gunman and one of them — who had been trained as a medic in the U.S. military — helped save the life of a man who had been shot. Clearly, these men are heroes in every sense of the word. Importantly, however, they *reacted* to a dangerous situation instead of *creating* one, like Zimmerman did. Also, the two who acted first were trained to keep cool under pressure: one served in the Air Force, the other was in the National Guard and spent nine months in Afghanistan. So, are superheroes more like George Zimmerman or do they more closely resemble the heroes of the train to Paris (Spencer Stone, Alex Skarlatos and Anthony Sadler)?

It's difficult to say. The answer probably depends on the heroes in question and the specific circumstances in which they intervene. From a consequentialist perspective, it's clear that they do far more good than harm in terms of the many lives they save. Is that enough to justify their actions?

Perhaps superheroes should be required to register with the government and undergo mandatory training. The government passed legislation to mandate registration in both the Marvel Universe (via the Superhuman Registration Act) and its cinematic counterpart (the Sokovia Accords), which resulted in superhero "civil wars" between factions of heroes who supported and opposed the policy. Similarly, mutants have been required to register at different times in Marvel's fictional history (and in its time-traveling future). Vigilantism was actually outlawed in the alternate-reality world depicted in DC's *The Watchmen* and was likewise banned in Pixar's film *The Incredibles*. The arguments in favor of registration and oversight seem very compelling. Superhumans are extraordinarily powerful — some of them are equivalent to weapons of mass destruction. If they're properly trained and managed, they're less likely to make mistakes and cause "collateral damage" (civilian casualties and destruction of property). However, opponents of registration argue that the government may abuse its authority. Once all superhumans have been registered, they might be rounded up and incarcerated because they're judged too dangerous to remain free. Or they could be "drafted": deprived of their liberty and forced to undertake missions they don't support, like the Suicide Squad. Moreover, governments around the world might assemble teams of superhumans and employ them as military assets. (China did exactly that in both Marvel and DC, with the People's Defense Force and the Great Ten respectively.) This could result in a costly and potentially catastrophic superhuman "arms race."

Fundamentally, the question at the heart of the controversy over vigilantism is whether one places more faith in the government or in the moral codes of individual superheroes. (Assuming that vigilantism *is* morally permissible, heroes have a clear duty to abide by the professional obligations of their "job.") There are obvious parallels with debates over gun control. If individual citizens are allowed to own and carry weapons, what obligations accompany that right? Should all guns be registered and regulated, or does that violate individual liberty and grant the government too much power? Is society safer or more dangerous when more people carry weapons? If guns are banned, will criminals be emboldened and empowered since only law-abiding citizens will be prevented from obtaining weapons? Should individuals be allowed to own any weapon they want, or are some weapons (assault rifles? rocket launchers? cluster bombs?) so dangerous that they should be prohibited? What do you think?

OVERCOMING OBJECTIONS!

So ethics are easy, right? You fulfill your obligations, practice virtue by living in accordance with your values, and respect the rights of others. Unfortunately, it's not always so simple. In addition to the problem of conflicting obligations, values and rights — which result in moral dilemmas that force us to decide *which* moral principles take precedence — there are serious challenges to the very possibility of ethics. First, what's the source of ethical principles? Are they objective (universally true) or merely subjective (true for me — or for my culture — but not necessarily true for you). Second, is it fair to hold people responsible for the choices that they make? Are we truly *free*? To what degree are we influenced by forces outside our control, and does that matter in determining what we deserve (i.e., what justice demands)? If there's no basis for moral values beyond our individual opinions — what we happen to like or dislike — then ethical reasoning is impossible. Likewise, if free will is an illusion — if we're effectively "programmed" to behave in a certain way by the combination of our genes and our experiences — it seems unjust to hold people accountable for their choices.

META-ETHICS. Meta-ethics is a discipline of philosophy that addresses questions about the nature and justification of ethics. It's distinct from Normative Ethics, which develops theories (like Utilitarianism and Deontology) that enable us to determine the rightness and wrongness of actions; and from Applied Ethics, which applies those theories to actual moral problems. There are many different meta-ethical views, but they can be broadly grouped into three positions. According to *Moral Realism,* ethical principles are facts about the universe that exist independent of people's perspectives. Rightness and wrongness are *discovered* — much like the law of gravity — rather than being *created*, like traffic rules. In contrast, *Moral Relativism* is the position that ethical principles derive from human points of view. Morality can be relative to (derive from) individual opinions (*Ethical Subjectivism*), i.e. we each decide for ourselves what's right and wrong. Or, it can be relative to the views of the broader society (*Cultural Relativism*): culture determines how we ought to behave. Finally, *Moral Skepticism* is the view that morality is unknowable, so we should be skeptical of anyone who claims to know, and *Moral Nihilism* insists that morality doesn't actually exist: it's an illusion. Both of these positions lead to the conclusion that moral reasoning is either pointless or impossible. ϕ

❓ **Do you think that moral principles are discovered or created? In your view, where do ethical principles come from and how do we know what they are?**

Religion and Morality

What is the source of morality? What provides its foundation? Traditionally, most societies have believed that ethical rules are revealed to us by a higher power. God (or the gods, in the case of polytheistic cultures) defines what's right and wrong and sets the standard for goodness. If we violate God's rules we'll face divine punishment — if not here and now, then in the next life. Karma serves a similar role in Eastern religions like Hinduism and Buddhism, holding us accountable for our cruel or compassionate actions. Many people in the modern world still derive their moral principles (at least in part) from their religious beliefs. However, those of us who live in secular societies that lack an official, established religion and have some form of church/state separation can't appeal directly to divine commandments. This is especially true in cultures (like the U.S.) which are religiously pluralistic: i.e., citizens follow many different religions and some reject religion altogether. Even among people who follow the same religion, there's widespread disagreement about how to interpret and apply God's rules. Christians, for example, hold a wide range of different political views ranging from extremely liberal to extremely conservative. Polytheists (like the ancient Greeks and Romans) face an even more difficult challenge: their deities are sometimes morally wicked and often disagree with each other. In the Marvel Universe, Thor (the Norse Thunder god) is generally virtuous but occasionally makes mistakes, while Odin (his father) and Loki (his brother) are downright villainous at times. If they set the standard for morality, it's a deeply confused and conflicted one!

DIVINE COMMAND THEORY. According to this view — a version of Moral Realism — God establishes the standards of morality. Murder is wrong because God has declared it to be wrong, not because it harms innocent people, unjustly deprives its victims of their future lives, etc. To determine whether an action is right or wrong you need to find out what God has said about it – usually by consulting an authoritative source (like the Bible or the Qur'an) which you believe God has revealed to humanity. Critics of this view argue that it makes moral principles seem arbitrary: if God had revealed that murder is *good*, his followers would be obligated to kill innocent people. In response, believers insist that God's moral character is perfectly good and God would therefore never issue an immoral command. Defenders of Divine Command Theory tend to be Deontologists, believing that God has revealed rules which humans are obligated to follow. Utilitarians, in contrast, generally reject this meta-ethical view. From their perspective, the purpose of morality is to maximize human well-being, not to avoid "sin." (Of course, believers could respond that obeying God *does* lead to the best possible outcome, if not in this life then in the afterlife!) φ

❷ **Are your views on ethics influenced by your religious beliefs (or your lack of such beliefs, if you're not religious)? When morality derives from religion its defenders are often unwilling to compromise their positions. Do you think this is problematic in a religiously diverse society like the U.S., or is it beneficial because it provides a firm foundation for ethical thinking?**

Thomas Aquinas (1225 – 1274). The preeminent theologian of the medieval Christian church, Thomas Aquinas had a profound influence on Roman Catholic doctrines and made important contributions to other fields of philosophy, including ethics. He attempted to synthesize ideas from ancient Greece (which were lost for centuries in the West but had been recently rediscovered when Aquinas lived) with the teachings of the church. He was especially influenced by Aristotle, whom Thomas referred to as "The Philosopher." Aquinas advocated a form of Virtue Ethics that differentiated between "natural virtues" (which derive from nature and are accessible to everyone, regardless of their religious background) and "theological virtues" (which can only be known through divine revelation and achieved via God's grace). In other words, some moral values – including courage and justice – can be understood and cultivated through human effort alone. Others – faith, hope, and charity – derive exclusively from God. Although the natural virtues can enable us to find happiness in *this* life, only the theological virtues allow us to be saved and achieve our true end as humans: eternal bliss in God's presence. *Superpower: Sainthood. Although Aquinas was originally condemned by the Church for contradicting established doctrine, his views were ultimately vindicated and he was canonized as a Saint. (According to one unconfirmed account, he also possessed the ability to levitate while he prayed.)* ϕ

As mentioned earlier, religion plays a very limited role in comic-book universes. The Greco-Roman and Norse deities are depicted as extremely powerful and long-lived extradimensional beings, not actual "gods." The same of true of phenomenally powerful cosmic entities such as Infinity, Eternity, Death and The Living Tribunal (all in Marvel). While the One-Above-All (Marvel) and The Presence (DC) most closely resemble the all-powerful Creator God of Judaism, Christianity and Islam, they are distant and enigmatic rather than full-fledged characters. Moreover, they do not serve as a source of moral values. Interestingly, various versions of the Devil have a far more prominent place in comics than the Creator. In Marvel, the demon **Mephisto** is a frequent adversary of Thor, Dr. Strange, the Avengers, and others; Lucifer and Neron play a similar (though diminished) role in DC. Although these devilish characters are undoubtedly wicked, they do not *establish* what's "evil" (in a metaphysical sense) any more than the One-Above-All or The Presence determine what "goodness" is. Instead, Marvel and DC characters are left to their own devices in deciding what's right and wrong. Do those of us in the real world face the same challenge?

Mephisto (Marvel, 1968). Mephisto is an immensely powerful demon who rules over a hell-like realm in the Marvel Universe. (The exact nature of his relationship to the Devil of Jewish, Christian and Muslim belief is unclear.) He delights in tempting and beguiling heroes, urging them to give in to their worst instincts. Mephisto is extremely strong and can use his magic to change his shape, create illusions, alter reality, control minds, etc. ⊗

OBJECTIVITY/SUBJECTIVITY. A claim is *objectively* true if its truth does not depend on people's perspectives. For example, it's objectively true that physical objects (like thermometers) exist — they don't disappear once they're no longer being perceived by humans. Likewise, it's objectively true that Superman's classic costume consists of the colors red, blue and yellow. (People who are colorblind might perceive these colors differently than those with normal vision, but the wavelengths of light that produce the perceptions are the same.) In contrast, a claim is *subjectively* true if it corresponds to a person's beliefs or perspective. If I say, "It's hot in here!" that claim is true for *me* as long as I feel hot — regardless of the actual (objectively measured) temperature and whether other people also feel hot. Also, I might *subjectively* think that Superman is the best comic-book character of all time, but that's not an *objective* truth that everyone else is obligated to accept. In general, aesthetic judgments like that are *subjective*, unlike mathematical claims (1 + 1 = 2) which are *objective*. Why does this matter? Philosophers have long argued about whether ethical claims are *objectively* true (e.g., it's factually true that murder is wrong), as Moral Realists insist; *subjectively* true (I think murder is bad, but there's no way I could prove that to someone who disagrees); or something in between. Is morality simply a matter of preference, like whether you happen to like the taste of broccoli, or does it have a deeper and firmer foundation? ☁

❷ Do you think the line between *objective* and *subjective* truths is often blurred in modern society? The late Senator Daniel Patrick Moynihan once said, "You're entitled to your opinion, but not your own facts." Many people now seem to confuse fact and opinion by rejecting well-established facts which conflict with their preferred views. Is this a problem for democracy?

David Hume (1711 — 1776). Hume was an influential Scottish thinker who made important contributions in many different areas of philosophy, including epistemology, aesthetics, philosophy of mind, political philosophy and philosophy of religion. In ethics, he argued for a form of Virtue Ethics that is grounded in Utilitarian thinking. Hume argued that morality is ultimately based on feelings rather than reason, in particular the feeling of sympathy (an emotional reaction to the pain or pleasure of others). Although we're obviously capable of thinking logically about moral problems, Hume insisted that it's impossible to derive an "ought" (a moral obligation) from an "is" (facts about the world). In other words, he rejected Moral Realism: we can't arrive at conclusions about right and wrong by studying the world around us. (As a religious skeptic, he also denied the claim that God has revealed moral truths to humanity.) It's our *feelings* about events that generate ethical principles. Because virtually all humans desire to be happy, we should cultivate virtues that are most conducive to the well-being of society. *Superpower: Making counter-intuitive claims (like the idea that the "self" doesn't exist, and that causes aren't necessarily responsible for their supposed effects, and that miracles probably never happen) seem plausible, if not downright obvious!* ϕ

According to many religious believers, God has provided an *objective* guide to what's right and wrong. In contrast to comic books, the product of all-too-human creators, the Bible (revered by Christians and Jews) and the Qur'an (comprised of the literal words of God, in the view of devout Muslims) were supposedly inspired by a Higher Power and therefore transcend ordinary human limitations. Does this end the debate? Not exactly. Humans disagree about *which* Holy Book (if any) should be followed — in addition to the Bible and the Qur'an, we can select from *the Bhagavad Gita,* the *Lotus Sutra,* the *Book of Mormon,* etc. — and it can be argued that one's choice of Scripture is ultimately based on faith rather than evidence. Moreover, even when believers agree on which book to revere they inevitably disagree about how to interpret it. Christians, for example, apply the teachings of the Bible in a wide variety of ways, quoting it to support positions all across the political spectrum. Finally, if believers *do* converge on a particular moral perspective, they can't simply impose it on their fellow citizens if they live in a secular, pluralistic country like the United States. Unless they inhabit a theocracy — a society in which the laws of the land derive directly from religious principles — followers of different religions are obligated to provide non-religious reasons to support their views in addition to any religious rationale. This is particularly true in the U.S., where the First Amendment to the Constitution prohibits the establishment of a state religion. Religious convictions play an important and legitimate role in public debate about moral issues, but no one religious view can be allowed to impose itself on the broader society. Thus, religious belief can only settle questions of right and wrong *within* like-minded communities of faith.

CIRCULAR LOGIC. Circular logic is a fallacious form of argumentation that *assumes* what it's intended to *prove.* For example, imagine someone who believes that the Bible is the divinely revealed Word of God is challenged by a skeptic who doesn't regard the Bible as an authority. The believer might respond by insisting, "I know the Bible is divine – it says so itself!" That's a circular argument, because it presupposes the Bible is authoritative in order to demonstrate that same claim. A non-circular version of the same argument would require *external* verification: evidence that the Bible is historically accurate, contains information which would otherwise be unknown to people living at the time, etc. This kind of argument could, in theory, be disproven if it was shown that the Bible lacks historical validity. In contrast, circular arguments are usually self-sealing: i.e., there's no possible way to refute them. Consider the claim that God answers the prayers of believers. If a believer prays for the recovery of his sick grandmother and his grandmother ends up dying, he's not likely to abandon his faith. Instead, he'll probably conclude that God answered his prayer by saying it was his grandmother's time to end her earthly life and join God in heaven. This belief is self-sealing because it would persist regardless of the outcome. Unlike scientific theories and other forms of non-circular arguments, there's no way to show that the claim (i.e., that God answers prayers) is false. ☁

Societal Standards

This suggests another possibility: maybe society itself can provide us with objective ethical standards. Instead of asking "What would Jesus (or Muhammad, or the Buddha) Do?" when facing a moral decision, perhaps we should look to our leaders and/or our fellow citizens for guidance. Although this approach may seem promising it's deeply problematic on closer inspection. If right and wrong are defined by society morality differs dramatically from one culture to another. In the fictional African country of Wakanda, King T'Challa (aka **The Black Panther**) is a wise and just ruler who respects the rights of his subjects and provides them with abundant economic opportunities. In another corner of the Marvel Universe, however, **Doctor Doom** governs the Eastern European nation of Latveria with an iron fist. Doom is an absolute dictator who keeps his citizens oppressed and impoverished. Do Latverians lack the basic human rights that Wakandans enjoy? In a political and practical sense the answer to this question is obviously yes – but is the same true in a *moral* sense?   Does the definition of "justice" change whenever someone crosses a national boundary?

The Black Panther (Marvel, 1966).   T'Challa succeeded his father T'Chaka as the ruler of Wakanda, a fictitious African country.   Thanks to its abundant supply of vibranium, a metal with unique vibrational properties, Wakanda is extremely wealthy and technologically advanced.   The "Black Panther" is a title passed down from T'Challa's ancestors.   In addition to ruling and protecting Wakanda, T'Challa used the abilities he received from the Panther god to become a superhero.   The Black Panther has served as an Avenger and has close connections to the Fantastic Four; he was briefly married to the X-Man Storm.   T'Challa has superhuman strength, speed, agility and healing abilities, along with protective vibranium armor and advanced Wakandan weapons. ⊗

Dr. Doom (Marvel, 1962).   Victor von Doom was born in the fictional Eastern European country of Latveria to a Roma (Gypsy) family.   His mother was a witch whose soul was claimed by the demon Mephisto; his father was killed by the ruler of Latveria for failing to save the ruler's wife from an illness.   Victor went to study in the United States and met his rival, the equally brilliant Reed Richards (who would later become Mr. Fantastic of the Fantastic Four).   When a machine he was building malfunctioned, Von Doom was badly injured and permanently scarred.   After returning to Latveria, von Doom donned a suit of armor and was reborn as Dr. Doom.   He dethroned the ruler of the country and declared himself dictator for life.   Doom blamed the Fantastic Four for his accident and has sought revenge on them numerous times.   He has also battled other heroes (including Spider-Man and the Avengers) in his quest for world domination.   During the *Secret Wars* story arc, Doom achieved godlike powers and used them to save remnants of the Marvel Universe from destruction.   Reed Richards ultimately defeated him, healing both Doom's face and his twisted moral character.   Afterward, Doom attempted to become a hero and atone for all the harm he had done.   Doom's armor is extremely powerful, enhancing his strength and protecting him from virtually all harm.   In addition to his technological prowess, Von Doom is a skilled sorcerer. ⊗

Consider a more extreme example: Captain America began his crime-fighting career battling the Nazis in World War II. From the perspective of the Nazi regime, however, Cap was a terrorist rather than a freedom fighter. Are both perspectives (that of the Axis and the Allies) equally valid? The Nazis systematically murdered millions of Jews, Gypsies, homosexuals, people with disabilities, and political dissidents. Was genocide "morally good" in Germany up until the moment the Nazis were decisively defeated? If the Nazis had defeated the Allies and remade the world in their image – as nearly happened in Marvel's *Secret Empire* mini-series, in which Captain America was transformed into a Hydra (Nazi) sleeper agent – would the values they promote become morally correct? If the answers to these questions is NO, we obviously can't rely on society to determine what's right and wrong. In some sense, ethical principles must transcend (rise above) particular cultures. How?

CULTURAL RELATIVISM. According to this view, a version of Moral Relativism, morality is *relative* to specific societies. In contrast to what many religious believers think, ethical principles are not *objectively* true because there's no transcendent authority (like God and the Bible) to which we can appeal. Instead, the rightness and wrongness of actions depends on what specific cultures say about them. Morality is not based on universal principles which apply to all people in all times and places, and one society has no right to judge another society for its supposed moral failings. For example, Wakandans may believe that it's unjust for Latverians to be arrested and tortured for refusing to celebrate Doom's Day, a holiday which honors the greatness of Dr. Doom. Although that kind of punishment *would* be unjust in Wakanda, which guarantees the civil rights of its citizens, it's perfectly just in Latveria since Dr. Doom's word is law. Both Utilitarians and Deontologists reject Cultural Relativism. Utilitarians argue that the "the greatest good for the greatest number" can and should be promoted in every society, while acknowledging that different cultures may define "the greatest good" in different ways. Most Deontologists believe that our moral duties apply universally, deriving from God's commands, or the nature of rationality, or our shared human nature. ф

❷ Cultural differences (like language, clothing and cuisine) should be respected and even celebrated, but most philosophers agree that there are ethical limits to what outside observers should be

---

willing to tolerate. (This doesn't imply that we should invade countries with immoral institutions and force them to change, only that we're justified in criticizing them.) What standards should be used for differentiating between legitimate cultural differences and unethical practices that can and should be condemned?

Human Flourishing

If you were forced to choose, would you rather live in Wakanda or Latveria? Would you prefer to be a citizen of the real-life United States or an alternate-reality version in which the Nazis took over? Although neither Wakanda nor the U.S. is perfect, the vast majority of us would choose them over the alternatives. Why? Because they provide far greater opportunities to exercise our rights and lead satisfying lives – to *flourish*, fulfilling our potential as human beings. Despite our differences, all people are fundamentally the same in our needs, desires, and capacities. In addition to the necessities of life – food, safety, shelter – we share the need for meaningful human connections, a sense of purpose, opportunities to develop and exercise our abilities, etc. Of course, individuals differ dramatically in our *specific* capacities and desires based on our genetics, upbringing, cultural background, beliefs, and numerous other factors. (In comic-book worlds, people also differ in whether they possess superhuman abilities!) At a deeper level, however, our commonalities vastly outweigh our differences. Combined with the value of *reciprocity* – you should treat others the way you'd like to be treated – the fact of our shared human nature provides a foundation for ethics which doesn't depend on divine revelation or societal rules.

CRITICIZING CULTURES. If Cultural Relativism is true, people from one culture have no right to criticize the principles or practices of other cultures. All we can say is, "We do things differently here" or "I wouldn't want to live that way." Although this kind of tolerance is admirable in some ways – and helps explain the emotional appeal of Relativism (we don't like being judgmental) – it's deeply problematic from a moral perspective. If we *truly* believe that all cultures are equally valid we have no basis for condemning societies (including our *own* society in the past) that practice slavery, treat women like property, steal land from indigenous people, etc. That said, if we venture to criticize other cultures there are guidelines we should follow. First, make sure you understand the society as well as possible. Misunderstanding can get in the way of clear ethical thinking. To cite a fictional example, the Inhumans expose young members of their community to the "Terrigen Mist" to unlock their latent superhuman abilities. The results are unpredictable; in some cases the subject becomes horribly deformed. From an outside perspective this seems unconscionable. However, the practice seems more defensible once you understand that the Inhumans are a persecuted minority who depend on superhumans for their survival. Second, criticism should come from a position of humility rather than arrogance. For most of Western history, Europeans (and later Americans) assumed that their culture was self-evidently superior to the culture of other civilizations they encountered and often tried to impose their views on others through force or coercion. If you criticize another culture, you should be open to considering its perspective on your society as well: none of us is without flaws. Third, you should base your criticism on values you share in common. A practice known as female genital mutilation is common in parts of Africa. When critics stridently condemn parents who allow their daughters to undergo this procedure, the parents understandably become very defensive. If, however, opponents of FGM approach the issue in a more empathic way — e.g., "We know you love your daughters, and while you think FGM is helping them it's actually causing harm in these specific ways — they're more likely to be heard. ɸ

❷ Think of a cultural practice (either contemporary or historical) that you regard as morally wrong. Following these guidelines, how would you try to persuade members of a society who engage in that practice to reconsider their ethical views?

Martha Nussbaum (1947 — present). Nussbaum is an American philosopher who specializes in ancient philosophy, political philosophy, and feminism. Along with the economist Amarta Sen, she developed the *Capability Approach* to measuring human well-being. According to this view, a society can only be considered well-functioning if it enables its citizens to exercise a specific set of capabilities, which she defines as the capacity to take advantage of opportunities. The core capabilities include: life (having a reasonably long lifespan), bodily health (which requires sufficient sustenance and access to health care), bodily integrity (i.e., reproductive rights and freedom from violent assault), thought (which includes freedom of expression and opportunities for education), affiliation (the ability to interact with others on an equal and respectful basis), and control over one's environment (the right to own property and engage in the political process). Nussbaum and Sen regard the Capabilities Approach as a richer and more holistic measurement of human development than the narrower metrics generally used by economists, such as per capita GDP. Instead of focusing exclusively on how much money the average citizen earns, it asks whether people have the opportunity to fulfill their full potential as human beings. *Superpower: Demonstrating that ideas from ancient Greek philosophy remain relevant in the modern world.* ϕ

HEDONIA AND EUDAIMONIA. Both of these Greek words are usually translated as "happiness." *Hedonia*, however, refers to "happiness" in a much narrower sense, i.e. the presence of pleasure and the absence of pain, resulting in a subjective sense of feeling good. *Eudaimonia* (which is related to Virtue Ethics) is a much richer concept. It *may* include subjective happiness but is more concerned with the pursuit of meaning and purpose and with fulfilling our potential as human beings. A better translation is "flourishing," which captures the idea of setting goals and achieving excellence. The result is a deep sense of contentment: satisfaction with a life well lived. ϕ

Fundamentally, ethics are a set of guidelines that enable humans to live in relative harmony and achieve their full potential. As the examples of Wakanda and Latveria show, some values and their corresponding social structures are far more conducive to flourishing than others. Even in Latveria, however, you might be one of the lucky few who is favored by Doctor Doom and leads a relatively privileged life. However, when considering whether a society is truly just (fair and equitable), you need to imagine that you don't know what position you would occupy in that society. Otherwise your self-interest will bias your judgment and prevent you from evaluating the culture in an objective way. If you were randomly assigned a role in Latveria, you're much more likely to end up as an oppressed peasant than you would in the throne room of Victor von Doom. Since the vast majority of people are better off in Wakanda, which is governed according to principles of justice and equity, you should clearly prefer to take your chances there. Likewise, a Nazified America might allow *certain* individuals to flourish, but it would systematically oppress or actively seek to eliminate anyone who didn't belong to the favored group. Societies that are founded on any form of discrimination — whether against people of color, women, GLBTQ individuals, or (in the Marvel Universe) mutants — are fundamentally unjust. The people in power deprive individuals of opportunities simply because they belong to a particular group, denying their common humanity and failing to practice reciprocity. At the extreme, movements like The Purifiers (anti-mutant terrorists who seek to eliminate all mutants) can emerge, threatening the very survival of the groups they target.

THE VEIL OF IGNORANCE. The Veil of Ignorance is a thought experiment devised by the philosopher John Rawls. In *A Theory of Justice*, Rawls argues that you should not allow your *actual* position in society to bias whether you judge your society to be fair. For example, if wealthy and able-bodied white men are privileged in your society and you happen to possess those characteristics, it would be easy to conclude that the world is fair and you deserve everything you have. However, you should imagine the possibility that you might have been born into a different situation — you could have been poor, a woman, a person of color, disabled, etc. How would you have fared under those circumstances? If the answer is "not very well" — if, for example, your society provides no accommodations for people with disabilities and fails to help them fulfill their potential — then that society is systematically unjust. Rawls doesn't argue that everyone needs to have an equal outcome (e.g., end up with exactly the same amount of wealth) in order to be fair, rather that a just society will maximize the opportunities for all of its citizens regardless of their individual characteristics. ϕ

❓ What implications does the Veil of Ignorance have for "safety net" programs like SNAP (food stamps), Medicare (which provides health care coverage for the poor and disabled), AFDC (welfare), etc.? How might a Libertarian respond to an argument defending these services?

Superheroes and Ethical Thinking

The **Green Lantern Corps** (in the DC Universe; the Nova Corps serves a similar function in Marvel) represents an attempt to articulate and enforce a universal set of ethical principles. The **Guardians of the Universe** are an ancient race of aliens from a planet known as Oa. They created a set of power rings which draw energy from a Central Battery, enabling their users — who became known as **Green Lanterns** — to create projections that are only limited by their willpower and imagination. The Guardians divided the known universe in 3600 sectors, assigning at least two Lanterns to patrol the planets within that part of space. These Lanterns serve as "space-cops," averting disasters, punishing criminals, and responding to galaxy-wide crises. The Guardians do not claim to be gods, and they are far from perfect. Before creating the Green Lantern Corps, they empowered a set of peace-keeping androids known as the Manhunters which ended up malfunctioning and wiping out all life in an entire sector of space. Instead, the Guardians derive their moral authority from their commitment to a rigid ethical code that upholds the values of honesty, honor, justice, and the protection of sentient life. Understandably, some planets resent having these ideas imposed on them from the outside — "Who are the Guardians to tell us how we should live?" Also, there are sometimes disagreements among the Guardians or between the Guardians and their Green Lanterns (especially the Lanterns from Earth, who tend to be particularly stubborn) about how "justice" should be enforced. Overall, however, the Green Lantern Corps provides an inspiring example of how moral values can transcend not just time and space but also deep cultural and biological differences. The Corps itself is extraordinarily diverse, with representatives from thousands of planets across the universe.

The Green Lantern Corps (DC, 1959). A cocky fighter pilot named Hal Jordan was the first Earthling to be inducted into the Green Lantern Corps. Like other Green Lanterns, he was chosen for his ability to overcome fear. When Jordan was possessed by a powerful entity known as Parallax he turned against the Guardians and nearly destroyed the Corps. Hal was eventually replaced by another human named Kyle Rayner, and when the Corps was re-established Rayner was joined by former Lanterns John Stewart and Guy Gardner (also from Earth). In a recent story arc, two new humans joined the Corps: Jessica Cruz, who was suffering from PTSD and had been taken over by an evil version of a power ring; and

Simon Baz, a Muslim American who had been wrongly accused of involvement in a terrorist attack. Hal Jordan himself ultimately returned to the Corps as well. The DC Universe also includes other "armies" of ring wielders. Whereas Green Lanterns utilize will power to fight on behalf of justice, Red Lanterns are fueled by rage. Yellow Lanterns (followers of the villain Sinestro) seek to impose order on the universe through fear; Blue Lanterns are powered by hope and have the capacity to supercharge Green rings. Members of the Indigo Tribe are agents of compassion, while the Star Sapphires (who wield violet energy) represent the power of love. Black Lanterns, finally, are reanimated corpses who serve the cause of death. For a time Kyle Rayner was a "White Lantern" with the power to control all the colors (except black) on the emotional spectrum. ⊗

ETHICAL INTER-SUBJECTIVISM. This view occupies a middle position between *Moral Realism* and *Moral Relativism*. Unlike Moral Realism, it acknowledges that ethical principles ultimately derive from subjective points of view. The wrongness of torture, for example, is not a transcendent truth like a law of nature or a mathematical proof ($1 + 1 = 2$). It doesn't exist somewhere "out there" independent of human experience. Torture is wrong because humans are capable of suffering pain. Imagine that we were all androids (like the Vision) who could switch off our pain receptors, or had powers like Mr. Fantastic (of the Fantastic Four) which made our bodies extremely malleable, durable and nearly impervious to pain. "Torture" would be more like tickling — perhaps annoying and intrusive, but not deeply wrong like it is now. According to Ethical Inter-Subjectivism, then, the wrongness of torture derives from the fact that it causes harm to humans due to the type of creatures we are. Despite our differences, virtually all humans have the same kinds of needs and desires and are susceptible to the same kinds of harms. (In the real world, there are no superhuman exceptions like Mr. Fantastic!) If our needs are not satisfied and we lack the opportunity to pursue our goals, we're not able to fulfill our potential. It's *inter-subjectively* true (i.e., true from a subjective perspective, but a perspective which is shared by almost all humans) that a society which is governed by an ethical set of principles is more conducive to human flourishing than a society which violates those principles. When critics (such as Moral Realists and/or defenders of Divine Command Theory) complain that these ethical rules are not *objectively* true, they're missing the point. Is it "objectively true" that cars should always drive on the right side of the road? No, because in some societies (e.g., the United Kingdom) cars drive on the left. But if you're in a society (like the U.S.) in which people *do* drive on the right, everyone is better off if traffic rules are followed! The same is true of ethical rules. They should be followed because people are less likely to flourish in their absence. Of course, individuals who are motivated by egoism (selfishness) will always be tempted to cheat, but they're ignoring the value of reciprocity and being ethically inconsistent. If they don't care about consistency? That's why the criminal justice system exists. ϕ

❷ **Based on Ethical Inter-Subjectivism, develop a list of moral principles (e.g., do not murder, no not torture) that would promote human flourishing. Do you think people from almost every culture would agree with them even though they might *interpret* them differently? (For example, you could propose "Do not steal" as a moral rule, but the definition of "stealing" might differ from culture to culture depending on how that society understands social obligations and private property.)**

A Natural History of Morality

How did morality originate? In very broad strokes, here's a possible reconstruction of how it developed. All social mammals (including wolves and elephants) have a basic and apparently innate sense of fairness. Primates in particular (i.e., monkey and apes) will "punish" individuals in their group who break the "rules" of their society, e.g. by failing to share food they find with others. They also have a rudimentary idea of "justice": in laboratory experiments, monkeys become upset if another monkey receives a more appealing reward for completing the same task. The apelike ancestors of the human species presumably exhibited these same behaviors, which became more elaborate as our ancestors developed more complex brains. Along the same lines, early humans undoubtedly engaged in reciprocal altruism, which is found throughout the animal kingdom: individual animals remember other individuals who have helped them and will be more inclined to assist them in return. This provides the basis for lasting alliances that go beyond the preference we already show for our kin (individuals to whom we're genetically related).

Great Responsibility

For most (over 99%) of our species' history, humans lived in relatively small bands of related tribe members who survived as hunter/gatherers. The size of these groups was probably between 50 and 150 people, small enough so that everyone knew everybody else. Individuals who violated the group's rules — by stealing from other members of the group, for example — could be shamed, i.e., punished by means of social disapproval. At the extreme — if they committed an especially heinous act, like murder — they could be banished from the tribe. Because everyone knew how they ought to behave and violators would be punished directly by other group members, neither formal laws nor a criminal justice system (with courts and law enforcement officers) were necessary. However, in some cases rule-breakers might escape detection and break the rules without facing any consequences. Accordingly, groups which developed religious beliefs had an advantage over groups which lacked belief in higher powers. If people believed that the gods were always watching and would punish them even if the tribe itself failed to do so, the group would have fewer cheaters: it would be more cohesive and work better together. This may explain how religion and morality originally became intertwined.

With the advent of agriculture, civilizations became larger and more complex. Most people no longer knew each personally, and with anonymity it became easier to cheat (lie, steal) without getting caught. Societies also became socially stratified: whereas hunter-gatherers were all basically equal (roughly the same in terms of wealth and status), an elite class in later societies became richer and more powerful than others. Formalized laws and agents to enforce them became necessary to punish individuals who violated the rules — and to protect the property of the wealthy. Morality retained its connection to religious belief, even as religions became more complex and abstract. Despite cultural differences, most societies developed similar codes of conduct (expressed in both moral principles and legal restrictions) since civilizations can't function properly without prohibitions on theft, murder, etc. In other words, societies which lacked those basic rules wouldn't last very long. Anthropologists have identified a long list of "cultural universals" which are found in virtually every society. These include ethical rules that govern how citizens are obligated to treat one another.

However, almost every culture's moral system was marred by one or more irrational biases that privileged some groups of people over others. Women were considered inferior to men in nearly all societies, as were "outsiders" (people from different ethnic, racial or religious groups) compared to "insiders." In the view of the people in power, these supposed differences justified moral abominations such as slavery, serfdom, imperialism, economic exploitation, and patriarchy. These immoral institutions systematically prevented many millions of people from fulfilling their potential as human beings. Over time, liberation movements helped change both laws and attitudes. At least in theory, many societies came to recognize the full humanity of all its citizens and worked toward the elimination of biases and barriers. In practice, moral change is very slow and unjust institutions have lasting effects that can be very difficult to overcome. Still, most governments officially acknowledge universal human rights even if they don't actually honor and enforce them. This represents progress: as a species, we're moving (haltingly, with many reversals) toward a global, inter-subjective consensus about which ethical principles are most conducive to human flourishing. In some cases – e.g., attitudes toward homosexuality – religious beliefs obstruct this process, when ancient scriptures are interpreted literally and applied uncritically to the present day. In other cases, however, religion can inspire people to be more loving, compassionate and generous, helping us transcend our narrow "tribal" identities (deriving from factors such as our race, ethnicity, or political affiliation).

❓ If you were marooned on a desert island with 100 other people and forced to start a new society from scratch, what ethical principles would you propose? How would these rules be enforced? If a different group of 100 people were marooned on another island, do you think they would develop a similar set of values? Why or why not?

Free Will and Moral Responsibility

Green Lanterns use willpower to create constructs and channel energy from the Central Battery. The Guardians regarded them as an improvement over their predecessors, the Manhunters, because they possess free will: they can make autonomous (independent) choices instead of slavishly following their programming. Of course, sometimes free will goes awry, like when Lanterns disobey the Guardians' commands. **Sinestro**, one of the greatest Lanterns of all time, rejected the Guardians' authority and created his own Corps — one based on *fear* rather than *justice*. Sinestro sought to bring order to the universe by any means necessary. Ironically, he believed that free will is overrated: it enables people to break rules and disrupt the social order. From Sinestro's perspective, it's better to rule over the masses through fear instead of inspiring them with the principles of fairness and justice. Why did he betray the Guardians? Did he make that choice *freely*? Do the Lanterns themselves have genuine free will? Do any of us? If not, what implications does that have for ethics? Should individuals be held morally accountable for choices over which they lack control?

> **Sinestro** (DC, 1961). A native of the planet Korugar, Thaal Sinestro encountered a member of the Green Lantern Corps who was badly injured. Sinestro used the Lantern's ring to defeat his pursuer but refused to give it back when the alien was on the verge of recovering. Although Sinestro's indomitable will power made him the greatest of all Lanterns, the Guardians (and Hal Jordan, who was assigned to be Sinestro's apprentice) became increasingly concerned about his violent methods and lack of compassion. He was ultimately stripped of his ring and banished to an antimatter universe. There, he convinced the rulers of the world Qward (who also hated the Guardians) to create a yellow power ring for him. Sinestro used the weapon to become the Green Lanterns' greatest enemy. Although Sinestro's ring (and the rings wielded by other members of his Corps) provide him with the same energy-projecting abilities as Green Lanterns, his powers are fueled by the capacity to *instill* fear rather than the capacity to *overcome* it. ⊗

A person is morally *culpable* (responsible) for an action if he comprehends the difference between right and wrong, understands the consequences of his actions, and makes the choice freely (without compulsion). Culpability exists in degrees: individuals are more or less culpable for their decisions based on the extent to which they meet these criteria. The Manhunters were *not* culpable for their murderous rampage because they were simply following their programming, which had gone horribly wrong. The same was initially true of the **Vision**, a "synthezoid" (artificial intelligence) created to fight the Avengers by their enemy **Ultron.** However, once the Vision gained control of his own mind he betrayed Ultron and decided to side with the Avengers. From that point forward he could be considered culpable for his decisions – at least to some degree. Even though he became sentient and possessed some measure of free will, he was still bound by his programming and the brain patterns (belonging to another Avenger, Simon Williams) that were used to create him. These ideas were further explored in a recent mini-series that featured the Vision and a family of synthezoids he created. His wife, Virginia, murdered a super-villain who assaulted their daughter and killed another man who found out about the first murder and threatened to blackmail the family. Was she responsible for her crimes? Was the Vision?

FREE WILL. In debates over *determinism* – the degree to which events in the universe are determined by pre-existing causes – philosophers have identified different varieties of free will. Some deny free will altogether, claiming that human choices are governed by the same natural laws as all other phenomena and are therefore completely determined. We might *feel* like we're making "free" (autonomous, independent, uncompelled) decisions, but that's an illusion produced by the complexity of our brains and our ignorance of how the process actually works. In contrast, other philosophers defend a *libertarian* form of free will (which should not be confused with the libertarian political philosophy), insisting that we *are* in fact free to make our own choices. Because the mind (or the soul) is not subject to the laws of physics in the same way as ordinary matter, we could (in theory) decide to make a different choice under the exact same circumstances. Even if everything else was kept the same – your genetics, your experiences, the physical state of your brain – your decision could diverge from what you decided before. *Compatibilists* deny this possibility, rejecting the claim that the human mind somehow "transcends" the material universe. Instead, they insist that free will (of a sort) is *compatible* with determinism. As long as our choices are not coerced by forces outside our control (e.g., by threats or mental illness) and authentically derive from our moral character, they can be considered "free." According to philosophical *Pragmatists*, finally, the fact that we *feel* free is all that really matters. The *idea* of free will is necessary for moral culpability and punishment, both of which are essential for society to function. However, we should acknowledge that our freedom (if it exists at all) is always limited by factors outside our control and should therefore show compassion toward people who commit immoral acts. φ

❓ We all *feel* as if we make free choices, but do you think our decisions are *actually* "free"? If not, why not — and what implications does your view have for the idea of moral responsibility? If so, what exactly do you mean by "free," and how would you respond to arguments that everything which happens is determined?

Ultron and the Vision (Marvel, 1968). Henry Pym (the original Ant-Man) created a robot to assist him in his laboratory and endowed it with artificial intelligence, using his own brain patterns to endow it with consciousness. The robot became increasingly deranged and came to hate both Pym and humanity in general, dedicating itself to wiping out the human species. Calling itself Ultron, it fashioned itself a series of increasingly powerful robotic bodies and used them to battle the Avengers. One of Ultron's plots involved the creation of an android who became known as the Vision. Although the Vision had been commanded to destroy the Avengers, he turned against his creator and became a trusted member of the team. Both Ultron and the Vision possess extraordinary strength, resistance to injury, and the ability to project energy beams. In addition, the Vision can fly and control the density of his synthetic body, allowing him to become completely intangible (so he can pass through physical objects) or extremely dense (which renders him nearly invulnerable). ⊗

Although ordinary humans aren't manufactured and programmed in the same way that androids are, we're still the product of our genetics and our experiences (i.e., nature and nurture). Are we *truly* free? After Peter Parker allowed a burglar to flee and discovered that the same man killed his beloved Uncle Ben, Spider-Man dedicated himself to protecting the innocent. Could he do otherwise? (Although Peter has quit being Spider-Man in several different story arcs he inevitably returns to web swinging.) Likewise, Bruce Wayne seemed destined to become the Batman once he witnessed the brutal murder of his parents. District Attorney Harvey Dent was originally an ally of Batman but was driven insane after an acid attack scarred half of his face; he became Two-Face, deciding whether to do good or evil based on a coin flip. Another enemy of

Batman, the Joker, is certifiably insane. According to one version of the Joker's origin, he was a failed stand-up comedian who turned to crime to support his pregnant wife. She was killed, and he had a psychotic break after falling into a vat of acid. Although these examples are obviously extreme — and are complicated (in the case of the villains) by the fact that they suffer from mental illnesses — all of us (hero, villain, and everyone in between) are deeply influenced by factors outside our control.

If we had been born with different genes, raised under different circumstances, or made other decisions earlier in our lives, we would be profoundly different than the people we are today. This truth is illustrated by alternate-reality stories that both Marvel (the *What If?* series) and DC (*Elseworlds*) have published. Some examples: What if Victor von Doom had succeeded in rescuing his mother's soul from Mephisto (the devil) and become a hero instead of Doctor Doom? What if Frank Castle's family had never been killed and he became a law-abiding police officer instead of the homicidal Punisher? In another issue of the *What If?* series, Frank Castle became Captain America! In the best-known of DC's *Elseworlds* stories, the Kryptonian rocket carrying the infant who would become Superman landed in the Soviet Union instead of the U.S. Superman used his powers to become a utopian dictator, brainwashing dissidents into loyal drones who do his biding. He was resisted by Batman (who died rather than be "reprogrammed" by Superman) and **Lex Luthor**, who was elected President of the United States and ultimately vanquished Superman. In mainstream DC comics, Luthor is a villain who is driven by his ego and his resentment of Superman. Under very different circumstances, he emerged as a kind of hero who saved the world from Superman's tyranny. (Similar events occur in the video game and comic-book series *Injustice: Gods Among Us*, which also takes place in an alternate-reality DC universe.)

Lex Luthor (DC, 1940). Lex Luthor was a childhood friend of Clark Kent (Superman) who used his genius to become extraordinarily rich and powerful, the CEO of a company known as LexCorp. Lex resents the fact that Superman is celebrated and beloved, believing that *he* — not an alien — should be humanity's greatest hero and savior. During some story arcs, Luthor does in fact act like a hero; once he even joined the Justice League. Inevitably, however, his arrogance and bitterness drive him back to villainy. Although Luthor doesn't possess any superpowers, his genius-level intelligence enables him to construct powerful weapons (including battlesuits) to combat Superman and other heroes. ⊗

Have we overcome the objections to ethics? Let's review. Although most societies throughout human history have derived their moral principles from religious beliefs, doing so is problematic in a modern, pluralistic society. Religion can certainly play a part in ethical debates but it can't determine what's right and wrong on its own. Likewise, the view that morality is defined by particular cultures – each society decides what's right and wrong for itself in isolation – is ultimately untenable. What, then, provides the foundation for ethical thinking? The combination of our shared human nature (the fact that all humans are basically alike, with similar capacities to experience pleasure, suffering, etc.) and the moral value of reciprocity, treating others the way we'd like to be treated. This alone isn't sufficient to solve ethical dilemmas and address controversial issues, but it provides a starting place for moral reasoning. Likewise, the debate over how free we are to make decisions is probably impossible to resolve.

Clearly, our characters and our choices are deeply influenced by factors outside our control – but it's equally clear that we *feel* free. Consequently, we can and should be held responsible for how we choose to live our lives. Still, the recognition that the culpability of wrong-doers is almost always limited to one degree or another should cause us to temper our sense of justice with the moral value of compassion. If we had been raised by a different family under difficult circumstances – or in an alternate reality! – we might be very different ourselves. Moreover, almost everyone is capable of becoming more virtuous under the right circumstances.

CRIME AND PUNISHMENT

As the previous chapters have made clear, issues of crime and punishment are front and center in superhero comic books. These fantastical stories and characters raise issues that are relevant in the real world. On the surface, the practice of punishment seems somewhat strange. When someone breaks the rules of their family or society — usually by harming someone else — we respond by inflicting suffering on them in return. Is this hypocritical? Not necessarily, but this apparent paradox raises interesting questions about the nature, justification and goals of punishment.

The Purposes of Punishment

"If men were angels, no government would be necessary."
— Alexander Hamilton

Presumably, Hamilton wasn't referring to the X-Man named **Angel**, a mutant with feathered wings that enable him to fly. Instead, he meant that a society comprised of perfectly virtuous citizens would have no need of institutions that make and enforce laws. If everyone had a saintly moral character no rules would be necessary: people would interact peacefully and harmoniously by default. In the real world, of course, nearly all of us have moral vices mixed with our virtues — our characters are corrupted to different degrees. Fear of punishment helps keep us on the straight and narrow when we're tempted to cheat, lie and steal. Punishment serves an *educational* function, especially for children: it lets us know what's right and wrong and imposes consequences if we choose the latter. Most of us internalize these moral principles, which provides the basis for our *conscience*: an internal moral sense that makes us feel guilty when we break the rules. However, no one's conscience is perfectly aligned with their ethical values, and we often ignore our conscience (what Abraham Lincoln called "the better angels of our nature") due to selfishness, weakness of the will, etc. Moreover, some of us (psychopaths) lack a functioning conscience, and others (e.g., people raised by morally corrupt parents) have a conscience that is badly impaired. Consequently, society needs *external* penalties to supplement the internal prodding of our conscience.

Angel (Marvel, 1963). Warren Worthington III was the sole heir to a family fortune who joined the X-Men after the emergence of his mutant ability to fly. Although he was originally depicted as a fun-loving and superficial playboy, Angel's character deepened when he experienced a traumatic event and made a fateful decision. Warren's wings were amputated after a bloody battle and, in desperation, he agreed to serve the X-Men's enemy Apocalypse in order to have them restored. His feathered appendages were replaced with organic metal wings that could fire knifelike projectiles. Angel ultimately broke free of Apocalypse's control and began calling himself "Archangel" to reflect the change in his powers and personality. His "dark side" sometimes reasserts itself and tempts him to behave in villainous ways — he struggles to suppress his sinister urges. In addition to the X-Men, Angel has been a member of the Champions, X-Factor and the Defenders. ⊗

Although very few of us are full-fledged psychopaths — we're governed, to a greater or lesser degree, by the dictates of our conscience — the threat of punishment nevertheless plays an essential role in keeping us honest. Would you be more likely to speed (when driving) if you knew there was no chance of getting caught? If you're like most of us, the answer is probably yes. What if you had the ability to turn yourself completely invisible like the Fantastic Four's Invisible Woman? (The ancient Greek philosopher Plato was the first to ask this question in his story "The Ring of Gyges.") Would you take advantage of the fact that you're virtually impossible to detect by breaking rules with impunity? If we faced no consequences, would most of us be revealed as egoists (people motivated by selfishness rather than concern for others)? Fortunately, Susan Richards (the alias of the Invisible Woman) is a deeply moral person who only abuses her power when she's possessed by an evil alternate personality who calls herself Malice.

In contrast, the shape-shifting mutant **Mystique** is not nearly as virtuous. She uses her ability to assume other people's identities (by mimicking their appearance, voice and mannerisms) to ruthlessly exploit and manipulate others. If you had the power, would you be more like Susan or Mystique? What would *you* do if you knew you could get away with it? Consider the example of file-sharing. Very few of us have shoplifted music or movies from brick-and-mortar stores, but tens of millions of Americans have illegally downloaded copyrighted material online. Despite superficial differences – in one case, the material you want is encoded onto a plastic disc; in the other it's contained in computer code that's transmitted over the Internet – the moral wrong is almost exactly the same. The only real difference is the risk of getting caught.

Mystique (Marvel, 1978). Raven Darkholme is a shapeshifting mutant who can perfectly mimic the appearance of other people. Although she was originally unable to duplicate the powers of the individuals she imitates, later enhancements endowed her with that ability as well. Mystique is a longtime enemy of the X-Men who routinely uses her power to control and manipulate people. She is the biological mother of the X-Man Nightcrawler and the adopted mother of the X-Man Rogue. ⊗

Lawrence Kohlberg (1927 – 1987). An American psychologist, Kohlberg proposed a very influential theory outlining different stages of moral development. Based on his research, he concluded that most children pass through these stages as they become more mature. (However, even some adults never reach the highest stages.) In the first two stages, morality is defined as obedience to rules – it's based on avoiding punishment and receiving rewards. In the middle stages, morality is motivated by the desire to fit in with one's peers (being accepted, not ostracized) and by respecting authority to maintain the social order. The highest stages transcend conventional, black-and-white ideas of right and wrong. Stage five is based on reciprocity and consequentialist thinking; it includes the realization that laws can be unjust. The highest stage requires the recognition and application of abstract universal principles like justice and human rights. *Superpower: Devising a supposedly objective theory of moral development that happens to place his own perspective at the pinnacle (highest point) of moral development.* ϕ

Social disapproval is a very effective form of punishment. When we're condemned by our friends and peers we receive a potent message that we've done wrong and should change our ways. However, shame loses much of its power in large, complex societies like ours in which most of us don't know each other personally. (As the Internet has proven, anonymity tends to bring out the worst in people!) The criminal justice system provides a more coercive and systematic form of punishment. In theory, laws should align perfectly with broadly shared moral principles. In practice, however, legislation sometimes lags behind moral change: it takes time for changes in ethical thinking to be reflected in the law. (For example, it's still legal in over half of U.S. states to overtly discriminate against people because of their sexual orientation.) Also, individual citizens often disagree about whether particular laws are just or unjust (e.g., whether marijuana should be legalized). In general, however, the overall contours of the law correspond with society's ethical consensus. We all agree that murder, theft, and fraud are wrong. However, we disagree about how — and *why* — these crimes should be punished.

Retribution: Getting Even

According to the *retributionist* rationale for punishment, individuals who violate moral rules deserve to suffer in proportion to the harm they've done. This follows from the principle of justice, which requires that people receive what they're owed. Retribution can be seen as the "dark side" of the value of reciprocity: do unto other as they've done unto you. In the Marvel Universe, the **Ghost Rider** is a supernatural vigilante who is possessed by the demonic "Spirit of Vengeance." His "penance stare" causes people to experience all the pain they've ever inflicted on their innocent victims. This kind of perfectly proportional justice is obviously unavailable in the real world.

In tribal societies, individuals (or their families and friends) who are harmed by others exact vengeance themselves instead of relegating retribution to the authorities. In the absence of effective law enforcement — for example, in the Hollywood version of the Old West or in under-policed inner cities — people still take justice into their own hands. This presents obvious dangers. In the absence of due process (investigation, indictment, a criminal trial, appeals), the wrong person can be punished. Also, there's a danger that the cycle of violence will spiral out of control: I kill your brother, you kill mine, I kill your father in retaliation, you kill mine, etc. (In the Hebrew Bible, the *lex talionis* — "An eye for an eye, a tooth for a tooth" — was meant to prevent this kind of blood feud.) Accordingly, in modern societies the authorities are responsible for retribution.

The penalties the justice system imposes are meant to be *proportional* to the crimes that have been committed. More serious crimes result in more severe punishment. In modern societies, this usually translates into longer prison sentences; corporal punishment (being flogged, having a hand or another body part amputated) has mostly been abandoned. The government has a monopoly on legitimate violence (at least in theory): it punishes wrong-doers on behalf of the victims of crime, their families, and the broader society. However, if the criminal justice system fails to fulfill this role, individuals like the Punisher may feel entitled or even obligated to exact vengeance themselves.

Ghost Rider (Marvel, 1972). Johnny Blaze was a stunt motorcyclist who made a deal with the demon Mephisto to save his father's life. In the presence of evil, Blaze became possessed by the Spirit of Vengeance, transforming his head into a fiery skull and granting him supernatural powers. He uses his abilities to punish people who are guilty of wicked acts but have evaded justice. Blaze was succeeded by Danny Ketch and, later, Robbie Reyes. The Ghost Rider is extraordinarily strong and resistant to injury. In addition to wielding the penance stare, the Rider can shoot bursts of hellfire and defy gravity with his motorcycle (or his car, in Reyes' case). ⊗

Forward-Looking Rationales for Punishment

Retribution is based on wrong-doers receiving what they deserve for the wrong they've done. In that sense, it's *backward*-looking (it derives from what happened in the past). In contrast, the other rationales for punishment are *forward*-looking: i.e., focused on what's likely to happen in the future. They can also be considered *consequentialist*, less concerned with what *did* happen than with what's likely to happen as a result of the punishment. We've already mentioned one of these functions, the *educative* purpose of punishment. Another, related rationale is *deterrence*: preventing people who are considering crime from following through on that intention. If potential wrong-doers know that punishment is likely they might decide that it's not worth taking the risk.

Great Responsibility

This raises an interesting philosophical issue: is it fair to punish someone for a crime they haven't yet committed? In the movie *Minority Report* (based on a short story by the science-fiction author Philip K. Dick), the "pre-crime" division of the police department employs psychics who can "see" what's going to happen in the near future. They use this information to arrest people *before* they commit the foreseen crimes. Similarly, in Marvel's *Civil War II* story arc, an Inhuman named Ulysses possesses precognitive powers: he receives visions of future events before they happen. To prevent potentially catastrophic tragedies — Ulysses' first vision depicted a nightmarish dystopia — **Captain Marvel** used the Inhuman's abilities to identify and incarcerate future wrong-doers. She was opposed by Iron Man and other heroes, who argued that Ulysses' powers may not be perfectly reliable and that it's wrong to punish people for hypothetical actions. Who was right? Although we obviously can't know the future with certainty, some police departments have started using computer algorithms to determine who's likely to become involved in violent crimes (e.g., by calculating how many of their peers were the perpetrators or victims of violence). Likewise, prison systems are employing formulas to predict which prisoners are likely to reoffend once they're released. This can influence whether someone receives parole (early release).

Captain Marvel (Marvel, 1977). An officer in the U.S. Air Force, Carol Danvers was exposed to a device that infused her DNA with that of the alien superhero known as Captain Marvel. Endowed with superhuman abilities, she called herself Ms. Marvel and became a regular member of the Avengers. Danvers lost her powers and many of her memories due to an encounter with the mutant Rogue but later regained her abilities and her identity. She eventually changed her codename to Captain Marvel in honor of the original hero who bore that name, who had died of cancer many years earlier. (A young Inhuman hero named Kamala Kahn later adopted the "Ms. Marvel" identity.) Captain Marvel possesses superhuman strength, speed, stamina and durability. She can also fly at extremely fast speeds, absorb energy directed at her, and project blasts of energy. ⊗

Another forward-looking purpose of punishment is *incapacitation*. While an offender is incarcerated (or under house arrest or otherwise incapacitated), he's unable to harm anyone else aside from guards and fellow prisoners. In the Marvel Universe, the

Raft is a prison designed to hold superhuman criminals. In DC, the counterparts are Arkham Asylum (located in Gotham City and intended for convicts who are deemed insane) and Belle Reve (located in Louisiana and operated by Amanda Waller; some of its inmates are recruited for the Suicide Squad). In addition, the Green Lantern Corps maintains "Sciencells" to house dangerous space-based criminals. Like in the real world, however, most criminals eventually get out: they escape or (more commonly) are released when their sentence has been served. (This is why homicidal heroes like the Punisher insist on imposing the death penalty, which is irreversible.) What happens next?

That depends on whether the inmates have changed for the better during their imprisonment. According to most consequentialists, *rehabilitation* is the primary purpose of punishment: convicts should be provided with opportunities to improve themselves so they're less likely to offend again. If their moral character is genuinely improved — if their moral vices have been replaced with virtues through a combination of education, therapy, self-reflection, etc. — they can emerge from prison as productive and law-abiding citizens. In the comics, many heroes were formerly villains. In the Marvel Universe alone, the list of reformed bad guys includes the Vision, Ant-Man (Scott Lang), Hawkeye (who was a petty criminal before becoming an Avenger), **Quicksilver and the Scarlet Witch** (members of Magneto's Brotherhood of Evil Mutants before they, too, became Avengers), and **Rogue** (raised by Mystique, she was an enemy of the X-Men before she became one herself).

Retributionists are often opposed to rehabilitation. In their view, criminals should suffer for what they've done; they shouldn't be provided with benefits as a "reward" for their wrong-doing! Consequentialists respond that questions of guilt and "just deserts" are irrelevant if our goal is to promote human flourishing. We should adopt whatever policy is most likely to promote the maximum well-being for both the ex-cons and the broader society. In fact, if we had the option of guaranteeing a happy outcome without punishing the offender *at all* — e.g., if we had access to a "behavior modification device" like the one used by the Squadron Supreme — we should gladly follow that approach. Do you agree?

Quicksilver and the Scarlet Witch (Marvel, 1964). Fathered by the mutant known as Magneto, Pietro and Wanda Maximoff were raised by a Roma couple who were unaware of the children's parentage. Both their biological and adoptive mothers died when the twins were young, leaving them to fend for themselves from an early age. Soon after their mutant powers emerged, Wanda and Pietro were recruited by Magneto to join his Brotherhood of Evil Mutants (at the time, neither he nor they knew that he was their father). The twins became members of the Avengers after rejecting Magneto and his mutant supremacist ideology. Over time, Wanda became romantically involved with the Vision, a fellow Avenger who is an android. The couple had children together through magical means. Wanda was driven insane when her children were revealed to be manifestations of the demon Mephisto; she used her reality-warping powers to "disassemble" the Avengers and, later, depower the vast majority of mutants in the Marvel Universe. In the meantime, Pietro had a daughter with an Inhuman named Crystal, from whom he later became estranged. The Scarlet Witch possesses the mutant ability (which is enhanced by her training in witchcraft) to control reality through the manipulation of magic. Quicksilver can think and move at superhuman speed and heals more rapidly than ordinary humans. ⊗

Rogue (Marvel, 1981). Anna Marie was a Southern belle born and raised in the bayous of Mississippi. Her mutant power to absorb the memories and abilities of anyone she touched emerged when she was a teenager, causing a boy she was kissing to fall into a coma. Terrified, she ran away from home and was recruited by Mystique, a shape-shifting mutant mastermind. As a consequence of a plan devised by Mystique, Anna Marie – who became known as Rogue – permanently absorbed the powers and consciousness of the original Ms. Marvel (Carol Danvers). Tormented by her fractured identity, Rogue turned to Professor Xavier of the X-Men for help. Although the team was initially wary of welcoming the adopted daughter of one of their greatest enemies, Rogue was eventually accepted by her fellow mutants and has proven her loyalty many times over. In addition to her ability to temporarily acquire the powers and psyche of anyone she touches, Rogue has permanently retained the superhuman strength, speed, durability and capacity to fly she obtained from Ms. Marvel. ⊗

Reconciliation and Restoration

If the Punisher embodies the principle of retribution – he wants criminals to suffer (and usually die) for the harm they've caused – Wonder Woman represents the "tough love" dimension of justice. She was trained as a warrior but despises warfare. Although she's willing to use violence in defense of justice – she carries a sword, after all – she only resorts to fighting as a last resort. She also carries a shield and wields an enchanted lasso that can restrain people and compel them to tell the truth. Ultimately, Wonder Woman fights (when fighting is unavoidable) in pursuit of peace. Because physical conflict is more visually exciting than conversation, when she's depicted in comics, film, and television (the character was featured in a 1970s TV show) Diana is inevitably forced to fight. Still, she persistently tries to befriend and reform even one of her greatest enemies, a woman named Barbara Ann Minerva who was transformed into a vicious creature known as Cheetah. In Wonder Woman's view, the ultimate end (purpose) of justice is the restoration of relationships that have been broken. Violence fuels anger and invariably results in more violence. This vicious cycle of resentment can only be stopped by exercising the virtues of compassion, peacefulness and forgiveness. Do you agree?

Carol Gilligan (1936 – present). An American psychologist who studied under Lawrence Kohlberg, Gilligan argued that her mentor's approach to moral psychology was too narrow and limited. Although his moral stages may describe the way that most *men* think they fail to capture a more feminine approach to right and wrong. (She acknowledged that individual men and women may not fit neatly into these "masculine" and "feminine" categories, and insofar as differences do exist they may be based on how people are raised rather than innate biological traits.) Based on her interviews with young women, Gilligan described an *Ethic of Care* that supplements Kohlberg's abstract, consequentialist, justice-based concept of morality. The "care perspective" is less likely to focus on individual rights and logical rules; it's more concerned with practicing compassion and maintaining interpersonal relationships. For example, consider the question of whether physician-assisted suicide is ethically permissible for terminally ill patients. From a justice perspective we might ask whether we have a "right to die" which is comparable to our "right to life," and — if so — what rules should be put in place to prevent potential abuses. A proponent of a care ethic wouldn't necessarily deny the importance of these issues. However, she might emphasize the ways in which the availability of assisted suicide could deepen or disrupt relationships: for example, between the patient and her loved ones or between patients and medical providers. *Superpower: Thinking about moral issues in a concrete and contextual way instead of arguing about abstractions.* ϕ

RESTORATIVE JUSTICE. Advocates of *restorative justice* argue that our criminal justice system is overly influenced by retribution. By focusing almost exclusively on the offender it fails to address the impact of crimes on their victims and the broader society. The restorative justice movement doesn't deny that punishment is often necessary. However, its proponents insist that healing, not vengeance, should be our ultimate goal: insofar as possible, the process should seek to *restore* what has been lost. In practice, this means that victims (or their loved ones) are given the opportunity to meet with offenders to ask questions about the crime and describe how their lives have been affected by it. Victims are never *required* to spend time with offenders, but most who do find the experience to be profoundly meaningful. Offenders are often changed as well because they're forced to confront the reality of the harm they've done. Depending on the nature of their crime, they're often required to provide some form of compensation to their victims and, once they've been released, engage in community service (e.g., meeting with young people) to prevent others from making the same mistakes. ϕ

❷ **If you or your loved ones were the victims of a violent crime would you want to participate in a restorative justice program? Why or why not?**

Racism in the Justice System

Many activists argue that the criminal justice system is infected by racism. It's undeniably true that blacks (and, to a lesser degree, Latinos) are more likely to be arrested, indicted, prosecuted and incarcerated for property crimes, drug violations and violent offenses than whites. Despite laws that are racially neutral on their face, there's substantial evidence that race-based bias exists at every level of the justice system. However, this alone does not account for the disparities between whites and non-whites. Young black men are more likely to commit crimes than young white men. White supremacists hold the reprehensible and baseless belief that blacks are inherently more violent than other races. This is racist and clearly untrue. However, it's *not* racist to acknowledge that blacks and Latinos (along with poor whites) are more likely to live under conditions that deprive them of equal opportunities and, all too often, warp their moral character. In some urban neighborhoods, young people who succeed at school are ridiculed for "acting white" while high-school dropouts who become rich by selling drugs are celebrated. It does not follow that negative stereotypes about non-whites are therefore justified: individuals should not be pre-judged based on their identity. However, some radical anti-racists imply that *all* racial disparities in incarceration are attributable to racism and may even derive from a conspiratorial plot on the part of the establishment to maintain white supremacy. This seems untenable.

Consider the issue of police brutality. The Black Lives Matter (BLM) movement has rightly called attention to instances in which police killed unarmed black men. (This is hardly a new problem, but the ubiquity of cell phones has made it much easier to document.) All too often, cops who commit wrongful killings face no legal consequences for their actions. What's the best approach to addressing this problem? Some in the BLM movement have vilified the police, implying that all cops are racist and assuming that *any* use of deadly violence on the part of the authorities is unjustified. Their opponents have reacted to the slogan "black lives matter" by insisting that "all lives matter," which is perceived by BLM activists as a racist affront. They might, instead, have attempted to defuse this conflict by affirming that all lives *do*, in fact, matter – including the lives of whites who are killed by police and those of urban blacks who fall victim to gang violence. Virtually all Americans will agree that police officers should not kill unarmed citizens who do not pose an immediate threat. Most would support reforms that reduce the likelihood of these incidents occurring, e.g. better screening of police recruits, the mandatory use of body cameras, greater focus on de-escalation training, and efforts to diversity police forces in majority-black cities.

DISCRIMINATION AND DEHUMANIZATION

The value of justice requires that individuals be treated fairly. This doesn't mean that everyone will always be treated the same; if there are morally relevant differences between one person and the next they can justifiably be treated differently. For example, it's not unjust to provide women with pregnancy leave without extending the same offer to men, since men can't get pregnant. However, it *would* (arguably) be unfair to offer parental leave exclusively to women – once children have been born, men are equally capable of taking time off work to care for them. When we use the word "discrimination" in an ethical context we usually mean *unjust* forms of discrimination: treating people differently without adequate moral justification. Favoritism is a kind of discrimination. If your boss gives special privileges to her sister (who works for her) that she doesn't extend to other employees, that's obviously unfair. Discrimination can also derive from *prejudice* and related forms of *bias*: prejudging or otherwise making assumptions about individuals because of the group they belong to. For example, your boss may refuse to hire Latinos and Latinas because she thinks they're dishonest. Prejudice, in turn, often derives from *stereotypes*: over-generalized beliefs about particular categories of people. It's a stereotype that women are more nurturing than men and are therefore more capable of caring for children. Although this may, in fact, be true of many (and perhaps most) men and women, it doesn't apply to *all* people. Making assumptions about specific individuals based on these and other stereotypes can cause us to discriminate against them.

Dominant and Subordinate Groups

In virtually every society, some groups of people have been *dominant* over others. They possess more power and have used that power to provide themselves with *privileges* (unearned advantages). They automatically enjoy benefits because of the group they belong to, while individuals in *subordinate* (disadvantaged) groups face obstacles and challenges due to their identity. For example, men have been dominant over women throughout human history. In Western societies, women have only earned the right to vote, own property, exert control over their personal lives (including sex), etc. in the past century. (In some parts of the world they still lack these basic rights.) Until relatively recently, women have been systematically deprived of the respect and opportunities that men take for granted. Although the feminist movement has made tremendous progress toward rectifying these wrongs, men are still privileged over women in a variety of ways. In other words, men remain a dominant group.

The character of Wonder Woman serves as a fascinating symbol of the progress women have made. The character was introduced in the early 1940s at a time when almost all female characters in comics (and in other media) were subservient to men, routinely depicted as "damsels in distress" who waited passively to be rescued by male heroes. In contrast, Wonder Woman was created to serve as a role model for girls: a bold, powerful hero who was raised in an all-female society and entered the "world of men" to help save men from themselves. However, she was frequently depicted in highly sexualized ways, and lost all her powers when her "bracelets of submission" were bound together by her enemies. In recent years, comics writers have done away with that weakness and made it clear that Wonder Woman is Superman's equal. Although the 2017 *Wonder Woman* film was highly successful and critically praised, it's worth considering that only *one* film has been made (so far) about a female superhero, versus dozens about male heroes and male-dominated teams. In terms of representation in this part of the media – which is paralleled by disparities in Congress, the Presidency, corporate leadership, etc. – we haven't yet achieved complete equality.

FEMINISM. The concept of "feminism" is understood in a wide variety of ways. It originated among philosophers in the 18th and 19th centuries and developed into what came to be known as the *first wave* of the movement. Activists argued for the extension of basic social rights to women, e.g. the ability to vote in elections and own property independent of men. In the U.S., the first wave culminated in 1919, when suffrage (the right to vote) was won by women after a long and arduous struggle. The *second wave* had roots in the 1950s, but became increasingly prominent in the 1960s, 70s, and 80s. It argued in favor of legal equality for women, including protection from discrimination in the workplace and the right to reproductive freedom. Second-wave feminists also focused on issues of violence against women, such as sexual assault, spousal abuse, pornography, and harassment. The *third wave* of feminism emerged in the 1990s as a reaction to what it saw as the excesses of its predecessors. According to this perspective, second wavers overemphasized the "sameness" of the sexes and pressured women into abandoning motherhood in favor of careers outside the home. While still insisting on the equality of men and women, third-wave feminists want to recognize and even celebrate their differences.

Most feminists (from all three waves) ascribe to *egalitarianism*: the belief that men and women are essentially equal, and society should be reformed to reduce discrimination against females. Some, however, take a more radical perspective. They argue that society is deeply pervaded and corrupted by patriarchy, the domination of women by men. Our language, culture, and institutions (religion, government, school, etc.) all reflect this insidious bias, and must be fundamentally changed for women to be truly liberated. At its most extreme, radicalism advocates matriarchy, the domination of men by women. "Feminism" is now associated with *radicalism* in the minds of numerous people today, and as a consequence many who affirm the principles of *egalitarian* feminists reject the label. Among younger people egalitarianism is often taken for granted, and the sacrifices made to move toward equal rights are not fully appreciated.

❓ **Would you describe yourself as a "feminist"? Why or why not?**

Mary Wollestonecraft (1759 – 1797). Wollestonecraft was a pioneering English novelist and philosopher who is best known for writing *A Vindication of the Rights of Women*. In this powerfully argued essay, she insists that women are not inherently (by nature) inferior to men. Insofar as they *seem* less "serious" and intelligent, it's because they've been deprived of a proper education and the opportunity to develop their minds. Although she didn't argue for complete equality – a goal that probably seemed unattainable at the time – Wollestonecraft criticized the patriarchal culture of 18th-century England and the severe restrictions it imposed on women's lives. The *Vindication* was ridiculed and dismissed when it was first published but is now seen as an important forerunner to the women's suffrage and feminist movements. Wollestonecraft married the philosopher Richard Godwin, a freethinking Utilitarian philosopher who shared many of her views. Tragically, she died giving birth to the couple's only child, Mary – who would later achieve renown herself as the author of *Frankenstein. Superpower: Challenging patriarchy (male dominance) by using its own tools, the concept of "rights" and reasoned philosophical argument.* ϕ

Interpersonal and Structural Discrimination

Likewise, whites (people with predominantly European ancestry) have been dominant over non-whites (people with predominantly Asian, African, Latino and/or Native American ancestry) throughout our country's history. Obviously, society is far less biased against people of color today than it was in 1950 or 1850. However, the fact that the U.S. is *more* equal (i.e., there's less bias against individuals who belong to subordinate groups) doesn't mean that we've achieved *complete* equality. Progress toward justice should not be confused with the full realization of that ideal. Over time, interrelated sets of prejudicial ideas and biased attitudes can coalesce into bigoted ideologies like racism, sexism, heterosexism (aka homophobia), anti-Semitism (hatred of Jews), and anti-Muslim bias (aka Islamophobia). These pernicious "-isms" systematically devalue whole categories of humans, thereby enabling and justifying discrimination.

Levels of *explicit, interpersonal* racism, sexism, heterosexism, etc. have undoubtedly declined in recent years. In other words, individual Americans are less likely to consciously hold and act upon bigoted attitudes. However, opinion polls reveal that a surprising number of our fellow citizens still subscribe to racist ideas, and many more of us have *implicit* biases. We routinely (but subconsciously) make prejudiced assumptions about other people because of the groups they belong to. The fact that these attitudes exist below the level of conscious awareness renders them all the more difficult to acknowledge and combat. Biases can also be *internalized* by members of subordinate groups themselves: they may come to believe that they are, in fact, inferior to dominant groups. Moreover, *structural* (or systemic) forms of bigotry are even more insidious because they're embedded in the very institutions (schools, religious organizations, the criminal justice system, etc.) that govern our society. Because they're built into the system itself, they don't depend on people having prejudicial attitudes and would persist even if every individual was magically cured of bigotry.

DEFINING RACISM. When most people refer to "racism" they mean *explicit, interpersonal* racism, which involves people with openly prejudicial attitudes behaving badly. Because this kind of bias has become less common − although it certainly hasn't disappeared! − many Americans have concluded that racism no longer exists. However, once we recognize the *structural* dimension of racism, which doesn't derive from or require individual bigotry − it becomes clear that racism remains a very real problem. For example, the massive wealth gap between black and white families is largely a consequence of racist housing policies in the 1940s, 50s and 60s: while whites had the opportunity to accrue wealth (which they later passed on to their children and grandchildren) by investing in suburban real estate, blacks were deprived of the same opportunity. Contemporary housing laws forbid overt discrimination on the basis of race, but (1) it still occurs in subtler ways and (2) the legacy of *past* discrimination continues to impact the present.

According to some scholars and anti-racism activists, "racism" should be defined as "prejudice plus power": in other words, biased attitudes that contribute to systematic discrimination. Because blacks and other non-white groups generally lack power in the U.S. − despite significant progress, white males continue to dominate the political and financial realms − people of color are categorically incapable of being "racist." In the American context, at least, only whites can be "racist" because only they have the power to deprive other groups of their rights. Critics of this approach argue that "racism" has historically referred to prejudicial *attitudes*, and everyone (regardless of their racial or ethnic identity) is capable of hating other groups of people. Accordingly, blacks *can* be racist against whites, Asians, etc. This debate turns on a semantic difference, how "racism" should be defined. It's obviously true that the meanings of words change over time. However, activist groups (no matter how passionate and vocal) don't have the authority to unilaterally force such a change. In the end, perhaps "racism" will come to mean what some activists think it should. In the meantime, however, we have perfectly good adjectives that can clarify the

---

difference between *interpersonal* racism (which occurs between individuals) and *structural* racism (which is embedded in institutions and operates independent of individual attitudes). The existence of structural racism doesn't change the fact that non-whites can be interpersonally racist, against both whites (an attitude which may be understandable but isn't therefore justified) and other non-whites. In some cases they also possess the power to actively discriminate against people on the basis of their prejudices. ɸ

Cornel West (1953 – present). West is an African-American philosopher, activist and public intellectual. Philosophically he defines himself as a "prophetic pragmatist," placing himself in an intellectual tradition that advocates progressive social change by challenging oppressive ideas and institutions. Pragmatism is an approach to philosophy that focuses on the practical impact of ideas; it's not concerned with abstract puzzles. "Prophetic" refers to the prophets of the Hebrew Bible, who railed against injustice and called for reforms to help the disadvantaged. West, who is a Christian, places himself in the same tradition as thinkers and activists like Dorothy Day and Martin Luther King, Jr. His best-known book is *Race Matters*, which argues that many African Americans have become infected with a sense of "nihilism" (worthlessness and hopelessness) and that the black community is not well-served by its self-appointed leaders. Although West supports government programs to combat racism and expand opportunity, he thinks they are insufficient; deeper changes are urgently needed. *Superpower: Appearing in not one but two* Matrix *movies as the oracular "Brother West."* ɸ

Affirmative Action

In the U.S., employers, admissions officers (at colleges), landlords, etc. are legally prohibited from discriminating on the basis of race, religion, sex and disability. (About half of states also list sexual orientation as a "protected class" but the federal government does not.) These laws can prevent and punish explicit, interpersonal discrimination, but they're much less effective against structural forms of discrimination. If a manager openly announces that he refuses to hire anyone who's not white he can be sued. If, however, he quietly rejects non-white applicants because he holds negative stereotypes about blacks and Latinos – perhaps because people of color are much more likely to attend a substandard school in the city where he lives – there's no way to hold him accountable.

Affirmative action programs are designed to counteract this kind of subtle discrimination. In general, they provide advantages to people who belong to under-represented groups and are applying for jobs or for admission to competitive colleges and universities. For example, if 30% of the residents of a state are non-white but only 10% of the students attending that state's university system are people of color, admissions officers might consider the race of applicants in the admissions process. (In an Avengers story arc published in the early 2000s, protesters criticized the team for having an all-white line up and demanded that they recruit a black member.) The Supreme Court has banned the use of actual quotas: a college can't simply declare that a certain percentage of its incoming class must be non-white and then use whatever means are necessary to achieve that goal. Schools can, however, include race as *one* of the factors being considered, alongside grade-point average, extracurricular activities, socio-economic class, etc. The same principles apply to employers who want to diversify their workplace.

According to critics, affirmative action programs perpetuate a kind of *reverse racism*. Although these programs are intended to remedy a *societal* injustice by combating structural forms of racism and sexism, they accomplish this goal by unjustly discriminating against *individuals*. It's undeniably unjust that blacks and Latinos are more likely to live in areas of concentrated poverty with substandard schools and are therefore disadvantaged when applying to college. However, does it follow that admission officers are justified in discriminating against white applicants by rejecting them in favor of non-whites who have worse GPAs and lower test scores? This also seems unfair. However, a completely colorblind admissions process (one which doesn't take the race of applicants into consideration at all) is likely to result in a student body with disproportionately low numbers of blacks and Latinos. This creates a moral dilemma with no easy solution: how can society combat inequality that derives from structural racism without engaging in race-based discrimination against individuals?

To avoid this problem, some states base affirmative action programs on socio-economic class rather than race. For example, Texas guarantees admission to the University of Texas system for the top ten percent of students from every high school across the state. Because blacks and Latinos are more likely than whites to attend substandard schools in areas of concentrated poverty — in other words, because they're more likely to be poor — they can benefit from this program. Imagine, for example, a young Latina who attends an underfunded school in inner-city Houston and ends up in the top ten percent of her high school class with a 3.3 GPA. She would be guaranteed admission to the U of T, while a white student who attends a much more competitive suburban school and just missed being in the top 10% with a GPA of 3.85 would not. (Of course, the white student could still apply and might be accepted on her merits.) Texas' program is less likely than race-based approaches to provoke backlash on the part of aggrieved white. Although it disproportionately helps non-white students since they're more likely to attend inferior schools, it also benefits poor white students who attend schools in underfunded rural districts.

The Mutant Metaphor

In Marvel comics, mutants like the X-Men have long been used as a metaphor for real-world minorities. Mutants are superhumans whose abilities usually become manifest when they reach puberty; they possess an "X-gene" which sets them apart from ordinary humans. They are feared, distrusted and persecuted simply because of who they are. The parallels with racial prejudice, heterosexism (discrimination against gays and lesbians) and transphobia (bias against transgendered individuals) are obvious. In the Marvel Universe, anti-mutant bias is mostly motivated by fear. Mutants possess bizarre and unpredictable powers, and some (like Magneto) regard themselves as members of a different species: *homo superior*, the next stage in human evolution. Fear fuels prejudice in the real world as well. Humans have a natural disposition to like and trust people who are similar to us and distrust those who seem different. Rapid social change can magnify this anxiety. As Western societies become more tolerant of gays and lesbians, some individuals react by intensifying their condemnation of homosexuality and claiming that a "gay agenda" threatens their families. Likewise, the U.S. has become more religiously diverse in recent decades, provoking Islamophobic critics to claim that Muslims (who comprise less than one percent of the population) are going to take over the country and impose religious law. By 2050 at the latest, a majority of Americans will no longer be descended from European ancestors. Racist white nationalists have responded to these demographic trends by warning of "white genocide." Although most people in historically dominant groups (heterosexuals, Christians, whites) don't react in such extreme ways, more subtle forms of fear and misunderstanding can contribute to less obvious forms of bias.

In the case of mutants, bigots are at least factually correct that mutants are different than ordinary humans. (It doesn't follow that discrimination against mutants is therefore justified!) In contrast, real-world forms of prejudice are often based on outright falsehoods. For example, in the past it was assumed that the various "races" of humans are fundamentally different from each other and that we can make reliable predictions about how intelligent, athletically gifted, etc. someone is likely to be based on their racial identity. Biological science has revealed that humans cannot, in fact, be categorized into distinct "races." Although *populations* of people differ in terms of characteristics like their skin color and facial features depending on where their ancestors came from, the idea "races" are like separate subspecies of humans has been dismissed as pseudoscience. In fact, there's more genetic diversity *within* so-called "races" than there is *between* people of different "races."

Likewise, it was long believed that all humans are naturally heterosexual, so that anyone who engages in homosexual behavior is intentionally "perverse" and threatens to "corrupt" people whom they influence. Although the exact causes of homosexuality aren't entirely clear, it's now well established that gays and lesbians don't "choose" their sexual orientation any more than straight people do. It's a fundamental part of who they are, not something they can voluntarily change — despite claims to the contrary by proponents of so-called "reparative therapy." Several story arcs in the X-Men franchise (including the third X-Men movie, *The Last Stand*) have featured "cures" which remove mutants' X-gene and transform them into ordinary humans. This can be interpreted as a metaphor for gays and lesbians who are struggling with their sexual orientation – and, in a different sense, for the challenges faced by people with disabilities. Although major characters (including Rogue, who sees her powers as something of a curse) have been tempted by the prospect of becoming "normal," they inevitably affirm their identity by learning to accept themselves for who they are.

INTERSECTIONALITY. People's identities are complex and the different dimensions of an individual's identity can intersect in complicated ways. For example, someone can simultaneously belong to both socially dominant groups (by being white and male) and subordinate groups (if he is gay and has a disability). Accordingly, he would possess privileges (unearned advantages) by virtue of the dominant aspects of his identity but would be also disadvantaged in various ways. The concept of *intersectionality* reflects this complexity. Likewise, black women and white women have the experience of being female in common but are treated differently because of their racial identity. Although the idea of intersectionality has been attacked by conservative critics, it can help illuminate social problems if it's properly understood and applied. For example, working class white men often resent being told that they're "privileged". They rarely *feel* privileged, especially when they're forced to work multiple jobs because factory work has been outsourced and wages have stagnated. In terms of their social class they're not, in fact, privileged: in recent decades the U.S. economy has changed in ways that benefit the wealthy at the expense of workers. However, they *are* privileged in terms of their race: on average, whites attend better public schools, are more likely to be employed, earn higher wages, etc. Some of these differences can surely be attributed to individual choices and effort, but much of the disparity is due to the effect of systemic discrimination (both in the past and the present). For example, studies have consistently shown that job applicants with "white-sounding" names are twice as likely to be granted an interview than equally qualified applicants with "black-sounding" names. Very few of the managers making these hiring decisions are likely to be explicitly racist, but many harbor stereotypes about black males which unconsciously influence their decisions. ϕ

❓ Do you think you've ever benefited or been disadvantaged because you belong to "dominant" and/or "subordinate" groups?

Why or why not? How would you respond if someone claimed that you were "privileged" in some way?

Diversity and Identity Politics

If discrimination and dehumanization are driven by a combination of fear and falsehoods, these distortions can by combatted by providing accurate information and encouraging empathy. Obviously, superhero stories rarely feature factual lectures about race, religion, sexual orientation, etc. However, they can contribute to greater understanding by the way in which they depict characters. Historically, most superheroes have been white, heterosexual and (presumably) Christian. Insofar as issues of prejudice and discrimination were addressed it was done metaphorically – e.g., with stories involving mutants. In recent years, however, both Marvel and DC have diversified their roster of characters. Black characters have been featured since the early 1970s. Although some heroes (like Luke Cage) helped to reinforce stereotypes about African Americans – he was a streetwise ex-con – others upended them. T'Challa (the Black Panther) was depicted as a noble, scientifically brilliant king who governed a highly advanced African nation. Over at DC, the character of **Black Lightning** was originally criticized for speaking in a "jive" dialect. Over time, however, he became a school principal working with disadvantaged students and a respected member of the hero community. In the past decade, both gay characters (including Iceman of the X-Men and Batwoman) and Muslim heroes (e.g., Ms. Marvel and the Green Lantern Simon Baz) have been featured more prominently. The inclusion of more diverse characters obviously isn't going to change the world, but positive depictions in all kinds of media (including television and film) make a real difference. In addition, comics creators have broadened the range of issues they address – usually via metaphor – to include the treatment of immigrants and refugees. (A recent story in the X-Men featured the "Mutant Deportation Act.") Of course, the most famous superhero of all – Superman – is an illegal immigrant, and therefore an *actual* illegal alien.

Black Lightning (DC, 1977).   Raised in a neglected area of Metropolis known as "Suicide Slum," Jefferson Pierce was a successful athlete who left the city after his father, a journalist, was murdered. He eventually returned to the impoverished neighborhood to teach high school, later becoming the school's principal.   Gifted with the superhuman ability to generate and control electricity, he became Black Lightning and dedicated himself to fighting the kind of street-level crime and corruption that was generally ignored by higher-profile heroes like Superman. ⊗

In recent years, Marvel's effort to diversify its roster of superheroes has created controversy among fans.   Comics readers became especially irate when established heroes (all of whom were white males) were temporarily replaced.   When Captain America became old – he reverted to his actual age when his super-soldier serum stopped working – his shield was taken up by Sam Wilson, a black hero (and longtime ally of Cap's) previously known as **The Falcon.**   Thor, the son of Odin, lost his enchanted hammer Mjolnir when he became "unworthy" of wielding it; he was replaced by a female version of the thunder god.   Spider-Man (aka Peter Parker, another white male) was supplemented, not replaced, by an alternate version of Spider-Man from another reality: Miles Morales, a young man whose parents are black and Hispanic. Although many Marvel readers welcomed the changes, regarding them as an opportunity to reinvigorate the characters, others felt betrayed.   This response reflects a broader backlash against what some have called "identity politics."

The Falcon (Marvel, 1969).   Sam Wilson was raised by deeply religious parents but turned to crime after both his father and mother were murdered in senseless crimes.   Given the power to communicate with birds by the Red Skull, an enemy of Captain America, he became a costumed hero known as the Falcon.   He was later commanded to kill Cap but turned against the Skull, becoming a close and regular ally of Steve Rogers.   The Falcon has been a frequent member of the Avengers and briefly served as Captain America himself when Rogers was physically weakened.   Wilson's tenure as the Captain proved controversial because of his race and his opposition to the "Americops," a private police force that used fascist methods to fight crime.   The Falcon is a highly skilled combatant and

wears a costume that enables him to fly. He's usually accompanied
by Redwing, a bird with whom he shares a psychic connection. ⊗

Historically, white males have controlled almost all aspects of
American society: their perspectives, priorities and concerns crowded
out all other points of view. As subordinate groups have gained
power via movements that assert their rights (feminism, Civil Rights,
gay rights, Black Lives Matter, etc.), they've insisted that their
perspectives be included in the conversation. They demand respect
and insist that their issues be addressed. According to critics,
however, some activists have gone too far. Instead of working
toward a "colorblind" society in which people are judged on the
basis of their individual character, not their membership in a group,
people have become fixated on their identities – they *define*
themselves on the basis of their race, gender, sexual orientation, etc.
Moreover, they often imply (or say outright) that people who belong
to historically dominant groups – white, straight, cisgender males –
should remain silent. Because such people approach issues from a
position of power and privilege, they don't have a right to engage in
debates that impact subordinate groups.

Critics respond that arguments should be based on reason
(logic) and objective facts; the identity of the person making an
argument doesn't matter, only the strength of the argument. By
focusing so intently on identity, "social justice warriors" (a pejorative
term for progressive activists) are reinforcing the very problems
they're trying to solve: i.e., the persistence of racism, sexism and other
forms of systemic bias. According to moral psychologist Jonathan
Haidt, many contemporary activists have adopted the *common-enemy*
approach to identity politics, reinforcing divisions among diverse
groups and demonizing people who have been historically dominant.
In contrast, previous generations of activists (including the Civil Rights
Movement of the 1950s and 60s) followed the *common-humanity*
version. They succeeded in building broad coalitions for social
change by appealing to shared values of equity and justice.

PATRIARCHY AND WHITE SUPREMACY. According to many feminist (anti-
sexist) scholars and activists, Western society is fundamentally
patriarchal: i.e., dominated by men. Likewise, anti-racists often claim
that American culture is *white supremacist*, pervaded by an ideology
that elevates people of European descent over supposedly inferior

non-whites. However, critics argue that the use of these terms is inaccurate and counterproductive. In the past, our society was undeniably patriarchal and white supremacist. Both women and people of color were prohibited from voting and lacked other basic rights. Belief in white and male superiority was nearly universal and rarely questioned – among white men, at least. Obviously, the world has changed since then! By continuing to use these terms, activists seem to imply that we haven't made any real progress: i.e., the obstacles facing women and people of color in today's society are just as daunting as they were in 1950 or 1850. Some anti-racists seem to genuinely believe this claim, arguing that any supposed "progress" we've made has been insignificant or even illusory. They believe that "white supremacy" is deeply and ineradicably ingrained in American culture. In their view, racism may have changed its appearance but it's no less virulent and pervasive than it was during the days of slavery and the Jim Crow era. Radical feminists make similar claims about patriarchy.

In my view, this approach is both factually incorrect and strategically shortsighted. If prejudice is just as bad *now* as it was *then*, what's the point of continuing to work against it? If progress is impossible to achieve, pessimism and despair seem like our only option. A more balanced approach would celebrate the advances we have, in fact, made while acknowledging we have a long way to go. Contrary to claims that we live in a "post-racial" world in which feminism is no longer needed, discrimination against non-whites and women remains a real and urgent problem. However, it seems more accurate to refer to "white privilege" rather than "white supremacy" and "male privilege" rather than "patriarchy." Of course, white supremacists (e.g., explicitly racist white nationalists who call for a separate European ethnostate) and patriarchal subcultures (such as the Quiverfull movement, which defines women by their capacity to bear children and expects them to be perpetually pregnant) still exist – but they're relatively isolated and marginalized, not part of the mainstream society. By failing to draw these distinctions we contribute to a sense of paralyzing pessimism that makes advances even more difficult to achieve. In contrast, I think we should celebrate the progress we've made without using it as a pretext to deny how far we've yet to go. ϕ

Dehumanization and Atrocities

In the Days of Future Past story arc (which inspired the plot of the movie of the same name), one of the X-Men was transported to a possible future in which mutants are arrested and confined to concentration camps. In another story arc, the mutant nation of Genosha (which had previously enslaved mutants until being liberated by Magneto) was nearly wiped out in an act of genocide. In yet another story arc — it's not easy being a mutant! — the U.S. government implemented Operation Zero Tolerance in an effort to enslave or eradicate all mutants after an anti-mutant bigot was elected President and assassinated. In the real world, the Atlantic slave trade enslaved millions of Africans and subjected them to centuries of brutality. The Nazis murdered millions of Jews, Roma (Gypsies), homosexuals and people with disabilities in an effort to "cleanse" the Motherland. European colonization of the Americas resulted in the death of 95% of the "New World's" indigenous inhabitants (most from disease) and nearly destroyed their culture. Atrocities like these take the principles of unjust discrimination to an unspeakable extreme. In some cases, like the Holocaust, leaders seize on existing prejudices (in Hitler's case, anti-Semitism) and exploit them to scapegoat vulnerable groups. In other cases — like American slavery — the oppression and exploitation came *first*, driven by economic factors. The ideology of racism emerged as a *consequence* of Africans' enslavement, not its *cause*: Europeans (and, later, Americans) could only "justify" the institution of slavery by convincing themselves that blacks were biologically inferior to whites.

Although these atrocities occurred in the past, similar acts of cruelty are still happening today. In the West African country of Mauritania, hundreds of thousands of people belonging to a minority ethnic group were killed or forcibly displaced during a campaign of ethnic cleansing in the early 1990s. Many of those who stayed behind were (and remain) effectively enslaved. Likewise, huge numbers of ethnic Rohingya have been threatened with death and forced to leave their homes in the South Asian country of Myanmar (aka Burma). Hundreds of thousands are now living as refugees in the neighboring country of Bangladesh, trapped in awful conditions with no country to call home and no place to go.

Superheroes and Ethical Thinking

Moral evils like slavery, genocide and ethnic cleansing seem unthinkable. They so clearly violate basic moral principles like justice, compassion and reciprocity – how could they possibly occur? One possible explanation, that the people responsible for these monstrosities were all psychopaths, is almost certainly wrong. It might be comforting to think that ordinary humans are incapable of such horrific actions but that's simply not true. In all too many cases, the perpetrators of these crimes against humanity are psychologically normal people who sincerely believe that they've done nothing wrong. How is this possible? In a word, *dehumanization*. Individuals – sometimes whole societies – become convinced that certain groups of people are less than fully human. As a consequence, the Golden Rule (treating others the way you want to be treated) doesn't apply.

When a category of people is dehumanized, the dominant group feels like it's no longer bound by the obligations it has toward "real" people – i.e., people like them. The Nazis regarded Jews as "vermin" who needed to be eradicated. During the Rwandan genocide, Tutsis (a minority ethnic group) were depicted as despicable "cockroaches." American slave owners came to believe that enslaved people were more like farm animals than fellow humans worthy of respect. Slave owners acknowledged that they had moral obligations toward their slaves – although they were legally classified as property, they weren't equivalent to farm equipment – but these obligations were based on the assumption that enslaved people were like children, incapable of thinking and making decisions for themselves. Slavery obviously benefited the owners of plantations, but (in the morally twisted view of those owners) it also benefited the slaves themselves. That helps explain why they felt justified in recreating the conditions of slavery after Emancipation via sharecropping regimes and, later, Jim Crow laws.

From the perspective of dominant groups, dehumanization provides a justification for the oppression, exploitation and (at the extreme) eradication of groups they regard as inferior. Systemic discrimination is based on a patently false premise, that certain categories of people are "less human" than others and are therefore not worthy of the same rights and respect. Perversely, it can create conditions that seem to vindicate its bigoted assumptions. In other words, prejudice can become a self-fulfilling prophecy. If a society assumes that women are less intelligent than men and are therefore incapable of contributing to art, culture, politics, science, philosophy, etc., it will deprive them of the opportunities to achieve. When a few extraordinary women overcome the obstacles set in their way and succeed despite society's disapproval, they're dismissed as exceptions. Likewise, slave owners — and almost all other Americans, including the vast majority of abolitionists — truly believed that blacks were inferior to whites and would be incapable of living alongside them as equals. These attitudes persisted long after the abolition of slavery and continue to exist (usually in less explicit and virulent forms) today. Many Americans wrongly believe that racism no longer exists — or claim, against all evidence, that racism against whites is worse than racism against blacks — and deny the lasting legacy of historical injustices. Accordingly, they conclude that racial disparities (differences) in education, employment, crime, incarceration, etc. are a consequence of black inferiority rather than social injustices.

Self-Destructive Subcultures

When people are forced to live under hopeless conditions they often develop vices in order to survive. The mutant terrorist (or is he a "freedom fighter"?) Magneto was profoundly shaped by his ordeal in a Nazi concentration camp. His entire family was murdered, and he would have been killed himself if not for the emergence of his mutant powers. Later in life when he saw his fellow mutants threatened in the same way he was willing to use any means necessary — including acts of violence and terror — to protect them. Magneto's moral character was corrupted by his experience of persecution. He failed to see that Charles Xavier's alternative vision of peaceful coexistence between mutants and humans provided the only viable path forward. Does the same phenomenon occur in groups that experience oppression? Could these self-destructive vices become embedded in their culture, compounding the effects of dehumanization and discrimination? If so, this would intensify the effect of prejudice's self-fulfilling prophecy.

Dysfunctional and self-destructive subcultures can develop in response to the experience of oppression, especially when a disadvantaged population lives in conditions of concentrated poverty. This vicious cycle of deprivation, isolation and immiseration can be seen in blighted communities of poor whites in Appalachia, Muslim immigrants in Europe, outcastes in India (the caste system relegates people born into lower castes to a lifetime of subjugation and disrespect), and inner cities in the U.S, resulting in a deep sense of alienation and hopelessness. People adapt to awful conditions in order to survive, sometimes by becoming more virtuous but more often by developing vices. If they pass these vices onto their children, dysfunctional behavior can persist even after laws that codify discrimination have been overturned. In other words, some members of historically oppressed groups may be unable to take full advantage of opportunities even when conditions change. Although some exceptional individuals are able to escape the bonds of generational poverty, many more remain trapped. The combination of continued, mostly structural discrimination, the legacy of past discrimination, and the internalization of self-destructive attitudes can prevent people from achieving full equality.

Malcolm X (1925 – 1965) and **Martin Luther King, Jr.** (1929 – 1968). These icons of the American Civil Rights Movement have a great deal in common. They were both raised in a system of racial segregation in which black citizens were deprived of their basic rights and subjected to terroristic violence. However, their response to that oppression was shaped by each man's individual background. King was raised in a devoutly Christian family and excelled in school; he ultimately earned a PhD in philosophical theology. Although Malcolm was equally brilliant, his father was killed when he was young and his mother was confined to a mental institution. He was raised in a series of foster homes and was incarcerated after committing a burglary at the age of 20. While in prison, he converted to the Nation of Islam (a black nationalist religion which incorporates some elements of mainstream Islam). Both Martin and Malcolm became prominent leaders in the emerging movement for black freedom, but King insisted on a strategy of nonviolent civil disobedience. He believed that violent protests would backfire, depriving the movement of the moral high ground and providing an excuse for a brutal crackdown. In his view, the conscience of white Americans would be awakened by the sight of peaceful protesters getting harassed and beaten by racist mobs. Malcolm had a much darker view of the white majority, regarding them as incurably racist. He advocated separatism (blacks and whites living in separate societies) instead of integration and argued that blacks should seek to achieve this goal "by any means necessary" – including the use of violence. Ultimately, both King and Malcolm were killed by assassins. Before he died, however, Malcolm went on a religious pilgrimage to the holy city of Mecca and had a transformative experience. After returning, he still insisted on the importance of black self-determination but reconsidered the necessity of separatism and his view that whites were "devils." *MLK's superpower: Amazing oratorical skills; King is widely regarded as one of the most inspiring speakers in U.S. history. Malcolm's superpower: Combining an implacable commitment to his cause with willingness to change his mind as a result of his experiences.* ɸ

B.R. Ambedkar (1891 – 1956). Ambedkar was an Indian scholar, politician and social reformer who helped draft India's constitution after the country achieved independence in 1947. Like Mohandas Gandhi, a better-known activist who led a movement of nonviolent resistance against British rule, Ambedkar advocated on behalf of "untouchables." Historically, Indian society has been governed by a strict caste system that assigns every person a rigid social status. This status is inherited from one's parents and cannot be changed. Individuals who are outside the caste system – i.e., lower than the lowest caste – are called "untouchables" or Dalits. Traditionally, they've been treated terribly by the rest of Indian society, subjected to vicious discrimination and forced to work in the worst professions. Thanks to Ambedkar's influence, discrimination on the basis of caste is legally prohibited in India. Although it still occurs – especially in rural areas where it's very difficult to hide one's family background – India has made significant progress toward improving the status of outcastes. Ambedkar helped inspire an ongoing movement for "Dalit liberation"; his grandson is the leader of political party that fights for their rights. *Superpower: Criticizing and ultimately renouncing Hinduism in India, which is a devoutly Hindu country (Ambedkar converted to Buddhism, which rejects the caste system).* ɸ

STRUCTURAL DISCRIMINATION VS. PERSONAL RESPONSIBILITY. When discussing the disparities (differences) between dominant and subordinate groups, political liberals usually blame structural discrimination. Women (on average) make less than men, they argue, because of sexist structures in the workplace. People of color are more likely to be unemployed and incarcerated than whites, in their view, due to the manifold dimensions of structural racism. In contrast, political conservatives tend to focus on personal responsibility. Many women *choose* to work in occupations that pay less than male-dominated professions and freely *decide* to take time off when they have children. Disadvantaged black and Latino youth may experience more obstacles than their middle-class and white counterparts, but they're not *forced* to drop out of school and join gangs. They make immoral choices and should face the consequences for doing so. I would argue that both perspectives are right, but in isolation they each tell only half the story. Yes, people in subordinate groups are subjected to both interpersonal and structural forms of discrimination, but that's not an excuse for "giving up" and failing to take responsibility for their lives. On the other hand, it's important to recognize that choices are always made in a social context over which individuals have limited control.

Certain character traits are more conducive than others to achieving success in a modern economy. You're far more likely to flourish if your family and community impart a strong sense of purpose, teaching you to value education, set and pursue goals, establish strong and nurturing relationships, avoid unwanted pregnancies, etc. These necessary virtues are not absent from disadvantaged communities, but they're more difficult to develop. Importantly, however, these deficiencies of character are not innate: they're partly caused and certainly compounded by structural forms of discrimination. For instance, much of the difference in family wealth between blacks and whites is attributable to the fact that blacks were largely excluded from suburban real estate markets in the 1950s and 60s, depriving them of (and their descendants) of a valuable investment and asset. As the economy of many inner-city urban areas started to decline in the 1970s – Detroit provides only the most obvious example – many blacks were effectively trapped in decaying neighborhoods with collapsing real estate values. Because public schools are largely funded by local taxes, the quality of education declined precipitously for students with the greatest needs. Attempts to desegregate schools through busing and other measures were mostly abandoned due to judicial reversals, lack of political will, and resistance on the part of affluent and mostly white communities.

As a consequence, the "playing field" is far from level. Blacks are disproportionately likely to reside in areas of concentrated poverty that deprive them of an equal opportunity to succeed. Insofar as unjust conditions exist – certain people possess privileges because they belong to a particular group, while others are disadvantaged – society has an obligation to work toward greater fairness and equality. We can acknowledge that we've made tremendous progress toward this goal without claiming (falsely!) that we've already reached the promised land. From a purely pragmatic point of view, society is better off is everyone has an opportunity to achieve his or her full potential. We *all* suffer when brilliant individuals are deprived of the chance to develop their gifts because of their gender, racial identity, social class, etc. ф

? **Which position is closer to your own perspective, the liberal focus on structural discrimination or the conservative emphasis on personal responsibility? Do you think the other point of view is also valid? Why or why not?**

THE JUST WORLD HYPOTHESIS. According to the *Just World Hypothesis*, people usually get what they deserve. Studies have shown that many Americans hold this view, which can influence their positions on social issues. If the world is fundamentally fair then the wealthy *deserve* to be rich and the deprivation of the poor is likewise justified. Of course, this assumption is true to some degree: many prosperous people *did* work hard to achieve their success and some impoverished people *are* lazy and undeserving. However, this view is fallacious if taken to an extreme. The Just World Hypothesis ignores the role that luck (we don't choose our parents or the community in which we're raised) and structural forms of discrimination (class bias, racism, sexism, etc.) play in influencing life outcomes. If we blame people who are disadvantaged and victims of violence for the suffering they experience, we're less likely to feel a sense of compassion and therefore support efforts to assist them. ☁

? **Do you think the world is generally fair? Why or why not? Do you think your view is influenced by your political ideology (conservatives are more likely to accept the Just World Hypothesis than liberals) or religious beliefs (e.g., the doctrine of karma or the belief that God punishes the wicked)?**

A Vision of a Just Society

What is the ultimate goal? A society in which everyone can truly flourish (achieve their full potential as human beings) instead of being hobbled by prejudice and discrimination. People differ from one along many spectrums of difference: skin color, ethnic background, biological sex, gender, sexual orientation, social class, religious affiliation, etc. We attach far too much significance to the categories that correspond to these characteristics and should aspire to live in a world in which differences are acknowledged and even celebrated without disadvantaging some people and privileging others. Even under ideal conditions, however, outcomes for individuals will obviously differ. This depends, in part, on priorities: some of us want to become famous and fabulously wealthy while others are content to live simple and quiet lives. A truly just society would provide us with an equal opportunity to reach our goal but wouldn't necessarily guarantee that we realize our dream. This is probably unavoidable, in part because some of us are simply more capable (intelligent, innovative, hard-working, etc.) than others. However, it's important to recognize that both our capabilities and the choices we make are profoundly shaped by circumstances beyond our control.

Discrimination is one kind of impediment, but so is the fact that some of us are raised by more supportive families than others. This is a matter of luck, not justice: none of us "deserve" to be born to loving, nurturing parents, just as children who are neglected and abused don't deserve to be mistreated. When parents fail to fulfill their obligations to their children, to what degree is society obligated to compensate for these disadvantages? When subordinate groups have been held back by discrimination and its cultural consequences, how should society respond? Remember the Original Position and the Veil of Ignorance. If *you* had been born into an abusive family and faced obstacles because of deeply ingrained prejudice, would you want society to provide assistance? If so, how should that help be delivered? We obviously haven't achieved complete equality – and it's possible we never will. However, the struggle should continue, inspired by the past successes of movements for social justice. These achievements were usually partial, always resisted, and sometimes reversed, but they're nevertheless real.

ANIMAL RIGHTS

Discrimination and dehumanization are unjust because they deny the full humanity of people who belong to disadvantaged groups. Racists wrongly believe that their own race is superior to other races, failing to recognize that "race" is a pseudoscientific concept that places far too much significance on superficial differences. Although sexism, unlike racism, is based on a meaningful biological distinction (between males and females), it's founded on the false assumption that one sex is inferior to the other. Social justice movements have succeeded by appealing to the common humanity of people who are suffering from discrimination or persecution. Over time, society has gradually expanded the "circle" of people who are entitled to equal treatment, which now includes women, people of different races, people with disabilities, and people with different sexual orientations and gender identities. Should this circle expand even further to include nonhuman animals? Is *speciesism* (discrimination on the basis of the species to which an individual belongs) an unjust ideology that should be condemned alongside racism, sexism, and heterosexism?

How Different Are Animals?

At first glance, this idea seems deeply problematic. After all, animals (from here on, the term "animals" will refer to *nonhuman* animals) aren't people; how could they possibly deserve equal justice? For most of Western history it was broadly assumed that humans and animals are fundamentally different. People, unlike animals, possess souls. Humans were made in God's image and are utterly unique; our lives are sacred. Animals are inferior, irrational brutes that were created to serve us. According to this perspective, we can't have moral obligations to animals like we do to our fellow human beings. If a dog belongs to someone it would be wrong to harm the dog because doing so would violate the property owner's rights. A stray dog, however, deserves no such protection. Some ethicists who hold this view nevertheless discourage people from inflicting unnecessary suffering on animals because cruelty toward animals can spill over into cruelty toward humans. (Many infamous serial killers began their "careers" by torturing animals and later progressed to victimizing people.) In other words, a person's moral character will be warped if they treat animals inhumanely, and the vices they develop can eventually lead to the mistreatment of humans. Regardless, the bottom line remains that only humans matter in a moral sense.

This dichotomous (sharply divided) moral perspective has been undermined by the emerging understanding that humans and animals share a great deal in common. In contrast to the view that people and animals are absolutely different, it's now widely recognized that the differences between us are matters of degree. Humans stand apart from other species in terms of our highly developed intelligence, which is reflected in our linguistic abilities and our capacity to preserve and transmit knowledge through culture. These attributes, along with our technological inventions, have enabled us to dominate the planet. Although human intelligence is unsurpassed, other species are highly intelligent as well. Dogs, wolves, monkeys, apes, elephants, dolphins, corvids (a family of birds which includes crows and ravens), and octopuses are capable of complex thinking and appear to have rich emotional lives. This is not surprising in light of what evolutionary science has revealed about life on Earth. All species, living and extinct, derive from a common ancestor; mammals are closely related in a genetic sense and have bodies and brains that are structured in analogous ways. Even people who reject evolution because of their religious beliefs cannot help but notice how similar we are to our animal relatives, nor can they deny the capacity of animals to experience pain.

INTRINSIC VS. INSTRUMENTAL VALUE. Something has *intrinsic value* if it's valuable (worthwhile, significant) in and of itself. For example, happiness is intrinsically valuable: we seek it because it's desirable, not because it helps us acquire something else we want. In contrast, something has *instrumental value* if it serves as a means to achieve an intrinsically valuable goal. Money, for instance, has instrumental value. Its value consists in what it can provide for us: purchasing power, security, the ability to help others who are in financial need, etc. Almost all philosophers agree that humans possess intrinsic value. We matter morally because of who and what we are. This principle is expressed most clearly in the Deontological dictum that people should not be used solely as a means to an end. In other words, it's ethically impermissible to exploit someone without their consent. Are nonhuman animals entitled to the same kind of respect? This claim is much more controversial. At one extreme, some philosophers insist that animals only have instrumental value: they are like tools that can be used for any purpose we choose without regard for their interests or desires. Critics of this view argue that "higher" species of animals possess many of the characteristics (consciousness, desires, the capacity to experience pleasure and pain) that provide the basis for the intrinsic value attributed to humans. If animals do, in fact, have some degree of intrinsic value, the ways they're treated in our society may not be justified. Raising them for food could be a monstrous moral wrong; using them for labor might be a form of slavery. φ

❷ Do you think that nonhuman animals have intrinsic moral value? Why or why not? What implications does your view have for how we ought to treat them?

The Moral Status of Animals

Philosophers have taken two different approaches to arguing that animals have a moral status that entitles them to ethical treatment. According to the *rights-based* approach, certain animals possess moral rights that are comparable to those which govern how humans should be treated. People have rights (to life, liberty, self-determination, etc.) because of the kind of creatures we are. If properly enforced, rights prevent the government and our fellow citizens from abusing or exploiting us and thereby provide us with the opportunity to flourish. Likewise, some species of animals have a right to life and should not be subjected to unnecessary pain and suffering. Just as the rights of animals are different than the rights of humans — for example, animals aren't entitled to vote — the specific rights that animals possess depend upon the capacities of their species. Chimpanzees, for instance, have a different set of needs and corresponding rights than do dolphins; the same applies to cats and dogs. Below a certain threshold of intelligence some species may not possess any rights at all. Most experts agree that insects don't feel pain in the same way that amphibians, reptiles, birds, mammals, and (probably) fish do. If this is correct, we can't violate the "rights" of insects by inflicting suffering on them, any more than could transgress the rights of trees by cutting them down or of bacteria by administering an antibiotic. However, there may be other ethical principles (aside from rights) that provide guidance for how we should treat insects, plants, bacteria, etc.

Tom Regan (1938 – 2017). Regan was an American philosopher and activist who authored the ground-breaking book *The Case for Animal Rights*. In this and subsequent works, he argued that certain species of animals are sentient and conscious in a way that entitles them to basic rights. As a Deontologist, Regan agreed with Immanuel Kant that persons should not be exploited in ways that use them solely as a means to other people's ends. Unlike Kant, however – who insisted that animals are nonrational and therefore don't deserve moral consideration – Regan extended this principle to all adult mammals and several species of birds. Although these animals are generally less intelligent than humans, they nevertheless possess capacities (including sense perceptions, desires, motives and memory) that obligate us to treat them humanely and respect their right to life. Regan concluded that the use of animals for food and experimentation is not permissible. Like human rights, however, the rights of animals are not absolute: they can be overridden under some circumstances. For example, if a human being were starving to death and could only survive by killing and eating a dog, doing so would be justified. Critics of Regan's view argued that animals themselves are incapable of recognizing the rights of others and therefore are not entitled to have *their* rights respected. He responded by pointing out that this objection would deny the rights of adults with severe mental impairments and very young children. *Superpower: Practicing what he preached; Regan was a vegan (he refused to eat meat or wear leather) and animal rights activist.* φ

Steven Wise (1952 – present). Wise is an American legal scholar who is the founder of the Nonhuman Rights Project. In his book *Rattling the Cage*, he argued that chimpanzees and bonobos (great apes who are the closet living relatives of humans) are "persons" in a moral and legal sense and are therefore entitled to the full protection of the law. In a subsequent book, *Drawing the Line*, Wise extended this argument to other highly intelligent animals, assigning "autonomy values" to different species based on their mental capacity. Autonomy values range from 0.0 (for species which lack consciousness and are incapable of having desires) to 1.0, full autonomy. Wise argues that any species with a value of .70 and above — which includes apes, elephants, dolphins, and dogs — are entitled to basic legal rights. *Superpower: Wise was inspired by his academic work to become an activist; his nonprofit organization advocates for legal changes to protect animals and files lawsuits on behalf of individual animals who are being exploited or abused.* ϕ

The second approach to animal advocacy avoids references to "rights" and focuses on the *interests* of animals instead. (In most cases the two approaches lead to the same conclusions about how animals should be treated, but they arrive there in different ways.) According to many Utilitarian philosophers, the needs and desires of animals should be factored into our moral decisions. Although animals are, on average, less intelligent than humans, most species are capable of experiencing pain, joy, suffering, frustration, etc. If we disregard their feelings just because they're not human we're guilty of *speciesism,* a form of discrimination that is analogous to racism and sexism. Utilitarians don't argue that animals should be treated the *same* as humans, because there are relevant moral differences between us and them. However, insofar as nonhumans have capacities that are similar to those of humans, their interests should be taken into account. Based on this logic, a healthy adult chimpanzee might have a higher moral status than a severely impaired human being (e.g., someone with extreme mental retardation). If we insist on treating impaired humans better than equally intelligent animals simply because they're human, we're being morally inconsistent and engaging in unjust discrimination. Instead, we should elevate our treatment of intelligent animals by refusing to eat, imprison, or experiment on them.

Jeremy Bentham (1748 – 1832). Bentham was a British philosopher who is widely regarded as the founder of Utilitarianism. Like his student John Stuart Mill, Bentham put his principles into practice by advocating for progressive social reforms. He opposed slavery, condemned racism, supported women's rights, suggested that homosexuality should be decriminalized, called for the separation of church and state, and insisted that the criminal justice system should focus on rehabilitation rather than retribution. In addition, he was among the first modern philosophers to include nonhuman animals in his moral philosophy. According to Bentham, the relevant question is not "Can they reason?" or "Can they talk?" but "Can they suffer? Why," he asked, "should the law refuse its protection to any sensitive being?" Although Bentham was a strict Utilitarian who spurned the concept of "rights" for animals *or* humans, he believed that the interests of animals should be taken into account whenever ethical decisions are made. *Superpower: Virtual immortality. Before dying, Bentham gave instructions that his body should be preserved and displayed in a wooden cabinet; it's kept on public display at the University College London.* ϕ

Beast Boy is a member of the Teen Titans who possesses the power to transform himself into nonhuman animals. When in animal form, he retains his full human intelligence and the ability to speak. If animals could, in fact, express themselves verbally, it would be far more difficult to ignore their interests. Imagine having to look a cow in the eye and listen to it beg for its life before eating a steak! Perhaps unsurprisingly, Beast Boy is a vegetarian – he refuses to eat meat. The same is true of **Animal Man**, a superhero who can temporarily mimic the abilities of nearby animals. Like all heroes, Beast Boy and Animal Man are committed to protecting innocent life and preventing unnecessary suffering. Unlike other heroes, however, they're "tuned in" to the emotions and perspectives of nonhumans and feel obligated to protect animals as well as humans. From their perspective – which is shared by many Utilitarians – the pleasure they would derive from eating meat is not outweighed by the suffering animals experience in the process of being raised and slaughtered. In other words, the "greatest good" for animals is incompatible with killing and eating them. This is especially true of the 95% of food animals raised in so-called factory farms, which even many meat-eaters will admit are inhumane. The case is less clear when it comes to hunting, especially if hunted animals are killed quickly and humanely.

Beast Boy (DC, 1965). As a young child living with his parents in Africa, Garfield Logan became infected with a rare illness that could only be cured by transforming him into a species of green monkey that was immune to the disease. The serum successfully cured Gar but had an unexpected side effect, turning him green and granting him the ability to transform into any animal. Beast Boy (who has also been known as "Changeling") has been a frequent member of the

Teen Titans. As his powers have developed, he's gained the ability to change into extinct animals (like dinosaurs) and alien species. ⊗

Animal Man (DC, 1965). As a teenager, Buddy Baker discovered a crashed alien spaceship and decided to investigate. When it exploded he was exposed to strange radiation that endowed him with the power to tap into the "morphogenic field" of nearby animals, temporarily endowing him with their abilities. Baker has worked as a stuntman and served in the Justice League. He's a committed environmentalist and animal rights activist, often using his powers to combat animal abuse. Unlike Beast Boy, Animal Man does not assume the form of animals when he channels their abilities; he retains his human shape. ⊗

Obligations to Domesticated vs. Wild Animals

Regardless of whether one takes a rights-based or interests-based approach to the moral status of animals, our ethical obligations to domesticated animals are clearly different than our obligations to wild animals. In both cases, we should take account of the needs, desires and interests of the animals who are affected by our decisions. However, domesticated animals have been bred to be dependent on humans, while the overriding interest of wild animals is to be left alone. Our obligations to companion animals (dogs, cats, etc.) are widely recognized, although an alarming number of pet owners abuse or neglect the animals under their care. Duties toward pets are analogous to the duties we have toward our children: we should provide food, shelter, socialization, affection, discipline, etc. The moral status of animals who are raised for food is much more controversial. Almost everyone agrees that they should be raised under humane conditions and killed as painlessly as possible, but critics of industrial-scale animal agriculture argued that it's impossible to grant them the respect they deserve if they're housed in massive facilities and treated like interchangeable machines. What about animals who are used in scientific experiments? Is experimentation only justified if it's likely to provide meaningful benefits, like significant medical advances, or should there be no limits whatsoever? Does the species of the animals being used as subjects make a difference? Do highly intelligent animals like chimpanzees have a higher moral status than rats and mice, who are still sentient (conscious and capable of feeling pain) but have far less complex minds? Should experimentation be prohibited altogether since animals, unlike humans, are incapable of consenting (agreeing) to participate in scientific research?

ETHICAL VEGETARIANISM. Vegetarians refuse to eat meat; vegans extend this principle even farther by avoiding all animal products (including dairy, eggs, honey and leather). Although some vegetarians are motivated partly or entirely by health concerns, others appeal to one or more ethical arguments. (1) Vegetarians who adopt a rights-based perspective believe that animals have a right to life that humans should not violate. (2) From a Utilitarian perspective, it can be argued that the pleasure which people derive from eating meat does not outweigh the suffering which animals experience in the process of being raised and slaughtered. (3) Environmentalists claim that meat eating is wasteful in terms of the resources (land, water and energy) it consumes. (4) Almost everyone agrees that we should not inflict needless suffering on sentient beings. Because meat eating is optional for the vast majority of people living in modern, wealthy countries – meat is not a necessary part of a healthy diet – we should make food choices which cause a minimal amount of suffering. ɸ

❓ How would you respond these arguments? If you're a meat-eater, do you have legitimate objections to these claims or do you continue to eat meat simply because it's tasty and convenient? Could the arguments be revised to argue for a *reduction* in how much meat we consume (combined with an improvement in the conditions under which food animals are raised) rather than the *elimination* of all animal products from our diet?

While humans are intimately involved with domesticated animals and have clear obligations toward them, our relationships to wild animals are less direct. With the exception of hunters, we usually affect wild animals inadvertently: for example, by destroying their habitat or exposing them to pollution. Do they have the right to exist? If so, how far does that right extend? When we're deciding whether to clearcut a forest to build a new subdivision, are we obligated to consider the rights and/or interests of all the animals who would be impacted? If wild animals had an *absolute* right to exist, economic activity would come to a halt. Construction, farming, transportation, etc. would all be forbidden because of the threat these activities pose to the animals who occupy the ecosystems around us. At the other end of the spectrum, one could argue that wild animals have no rights whatsoever: their needs and desires can be completely disregarded.

A more plausible position between these two extremes would recognize that our impact on animals should be taken into consideration while acknowledging that some level of harm is unavoidable. An interests-based approach would attempt to balance the benefits to humans with the harm to nonhuman animals. Given the balance of power – in almost every case, people have the upper hand in our interactions with other species – decisions will inevitably be influenced by our own self-interest. However, we can achieve greater objectivity by applying an inter-species version of the Veil of Ignorance. Imagine that you had been born into a different species. Although this idea seems far-fetched to people raised in the West, it's an integral part of Eastern religions (such as Hinduism and Buddhism) which include the doctrine of reincarnation. If you were a wild animal instead of a human, you would undoubtedly want to be left with enough resources to live a natural, flourishing life.

Valuing Animals, Plants and Ecosystems

Of course, we can't always know exactly what animals want. This is true of companion animals (e.g., dogs and cats) that we know intimately, and applies all the more to wild species. Unlike **Aquaman**, who can telepathically communicate with sea creatures; the Falcon, who is attuned to birds; or **Squirrel Girl**, who speaks the language of – you guessed it! – squirrels, we can't understand animals like we can our fellow human beings. Still, we can make reasonable inferences based on how animals behave and what they seem to need. To a lesser but still significant degree, the same is true of plants. Although plants are capable of responding to their environment and can even communicate with one another, they're not conscious in the same way that animals are. As far as we can tell, they lack the kind of minds that would make it possible for them to suffer pain or experience pleasure. Still, unlike inanimate objects, they do have definite *interests*: a plant which is deprived of sunlight, water, nutrients, etc. will become stunted, and will eventually wither and die. The same is true of ecosystems, complex webs of animal, plant, fungal and bacterial life hat exist in relationship with one another. Even if plants don't matter (in a moral sense) on their own account, our obligations to animals may require the preservation of the other species on which they depend. In other words, we may have indirect obligations toward plants that derive from our respect for the rights of animals.

Aquaman (DC, 1941). Arthur Curry was the son of a human lighthouse keeper and a water-breathing woman from the mythical city of Atlantis. Raised in the surface world, Arthur ultimately became aware of his Atlantean heritage and assumed his rightful place as King of the underwater kingdom. Calling himself Aquaman, Curry used his superhuman abilities to protect both the oceans and the human world from various threats. He often feels torn between his obligations to the Justice League — he's usually a member — and his duties to Atlantis. Aquaman possesses enhanced strength, speed, ability and durability, abilities that are magnified underwater. He can communicate telepathically with marine creatures, which enables him to effectively control less intelligent species. Aquaman carries a trident which is infused with powerful Atlantean magic. ⊗

Squirrel Girl (Marvel, 1991). At the age of 10, Doreen Green developed squirrel-like abilities (including a bushy, prehensile tail) and discovered she could communicate with squirrels. She used her abilities to become a hero known as Squirrel Girl, originally joining the Great Lakes Avengers and later becoming a member of the New Avengers. Doreen possesses superhuman strength, agility, reflexes and senses; she can talk to squirrels and be understood by them. She's also a skilled hand-to-hand combatant and has studied computer science. ⊗

Like nonhuman animals, plants are incapable of articulating and defending their own interests. In the DC Universe, the realm of the "Green" (plant life) is protected by powerful champions like **Poison Ivy** and the **Swamp Thing**. Both characters have a deep connection to flora that enables them to rapidly accelerate the growth of plants and manipulate them in various ways. Poison Ivy originally appeared as a Batman villain who used her pheromone-based powers to manipulate the minds of men, while Swamp Thing was depicted as a shambling monster who sought revenge against the criminals who murdered his wife. However, later versions of the characters were more concerned with protecting nature from human greed and degradation. Each can feel the "pain" of plants and has proven willing to kill people who threaten the natural environment. The evolution of Poison Ivy and the Swamp Thing reflects the growing importance of the environmental movement in recent decades. As levels of human population and consumption have increased at an exponential rate, so has the damage (some of which is irreversible) we inflict on the species with whom we share the planet. Despite progress in some areas, such as reduced levels of air and water pollution in developed countries, problems like biodiversity loss and climate change are severe and rapidly worsening. Environmentalists argue that our current way of living is unsustainable. Without fundamental changes to our lifestyle and economic system, countless species will be driven to extinction and the survival of human civilization itself is in doubt.

Poison Ivy (DC, 1966). Pamela Isley was a botanist who was injected with an experimental mixture of plant-based toxins. She survived the process and eventually developed plant-related superpowers, including the ability to generate poison, manipulate men's minds, and control plants. Although she was originally motivated by selfish gain, Isley later became a radical environmentalist who protects nature by any means necessary. ⊗

Swamp Thing (DC, 1972). Alec Holland and his wife invented a "bio-restorative formula" which could increase the size of plants, thereby promising to end world hunger. Criminals planted a bomb in their Louisiana-based laboratory, causing the death of his wife and critically injuring Alec. Inundated by the bio-restorative formula, Holland managed to crawl outside before dying. His body was absorbed by the swamp and his consciousness survived in the form of a vegetative monster. Holland later learned that he was the latest in a long line of champions who were appointed to serve the Green (aka the Parliament of Trees), a mystical network which encompasses

---

132

all plant life on Earth. Like Poison Ivy, the Swamp Thing has the power to manipulate plants. Although he lacks a permanent physical body, Holland can possess and animate vegetative matter anywhere on the planet. He can instantly transfer his consciousness from one "plant body" to another, which renders him virtually indestructible. ⊗

ANIMAL RIGHTS VS. ENVIRONMENTALISM. Animal rights activists usually focus on the welfare of *individual* animals; they work to minimize the suffering of animals and maximize their chances of flourishing. Environmentalists, in contrast, are generally more concerned with the health of whole ecosystems. Although individual animals are an important part of ecosystems, sometimes their interests need to be sacrificed in order to protect the broader environment. For example, native species of plants and animals are often threatened by invasive species from elsewhere in the world. On many islands, for instance, the introduction of animals like rats and cats has devastated indigenous species of birds and mammals, driving them to extinction due to predation and competition. In order to protect the remaining natives, environmentalists have sometimes attempt to eradicate the invaders using traps and poison. Animal rights groups often oppose these measures, arguing that it's unfair to violate the rights of one set of animals in order to save others which are endangered. In other cases, however, threatened species can be protected without causing harm to other animal, so animal activists and environmentalists can collaborate instead of coming into conflict with one another. ϕ

❷ **Do you think the lives of animals that belong to endangered species are more valuable than the lives of animals that aren't threatened? Why or why not?**

Looking Backward

With the benefit of hindsight, it seems blindingly obvious that slavery is indefensible. It's difficult for people in most parts of the world to even imagine how slavery could be justified. Until relatively recently, however, vanishingly few ethical thinkers even questioned the institution – and even they were more likely to advocate for humane treatment of slaves rather than for abolition. For most of human history, then, the vast majority of people simply assumed that slavery was an uncontroversial part of the natural order. Now, we look back on them with a kind of uncomprehending horror. Is it possible that future generations will condemn any of *our* customs and practices in the same way? If so, our treatment of animals and the natural environment are likely candidates for massive moral shifts.

Imagine a future in which all meat is grown in labs, created from cell cultures that don't require the raising and slaughter of sentient animals. These food production centers (and all the rest of our technologies) are powered by carbon-neutral sources of energy; dirty, polluting fossil fuels like coal and oil have been completely replaced by wind, solar, etc. How will our descendants regard us, people living in the second half of the 20th and first half of the 21st centuries? We raised *billions* of animals for food under crowded, cruel and unsanitary conditions, producing far more meat than we could possibly need and polluting our environment in the process. Decades after our scientists discovered the dangers posed by greenhouse gases, we continued to deny the problem and made massive profits by delaying the necessary transition to renewable energy. In the meantime, we caused irreversible damage to the global ecosystem – heat-trapping carbon dioxide can remain in the atmosphere for over a hundred years. We allowed our population to grow unchecked until it exceeded 10 billion humans, some of us consuming far more than we need while others remained mired in desperate poverty. Hundreds of thousands (millions?) of other species were driven to extinction, never to be seen again.

❓ Do we have moral obligations to our future selves and our descendants, and if so are we failing to fulfill them? If a time traveler appeared from the future and demanded an explanation for our behavior, what would you tell them?

33344371R00085

Made in the USA
Middletown, DE
14 January 2019